PRACTICE

VOYAGES
IN ENGLISH
GRAMMAR AND WRITING

LOYOLAPRESS.

Cover Design: Kathryn Seckman
Cover Art: Carrie Gowran
Interior Design: Think Book Works

ISBN-13: 978-0-8294-4309-7
ISBN-10: 0-8294-4309-6

LOYOLA PRESS.
3441 N. Ashland Avenue
Chicago, Illinois 60657
(800) 621-1008
www.loyolapress.com

19 20 21 22 23 LSC 10 9 8 7 6 5 4 3

Contents

GRAMMAR

WRITING

WRITTEN AND ORAL COMMUNICATIONS

1.2 More Singular and Plural Nouns

Most **plural nouns** are formed by adding -*s*. Some plurals are formed by adding -*es*. Some plurals have spelling changes but do not add -*s* or -*es*. Other plurals do not change from their singular forms.

Underline each singular noun once. Underline each plural noun twice.

1. Did you untangle your hair with the green comb?

2. I will make your copies after I finish printing these.

3. Raul prefers plain water, but Gabriel's drink is orange juice.

4. Check these problems because these numbers do not make sense.

5. The green apple in the basket will last the longest.

Complete each sentence with the plural form of the noun in parenthesis.

6. Amy Tan was born in Oakland, California, to Chinese-born _____ (parent).

7. She is the author of many _____ (story) and _____ (novel).

8. Ms. Tan's books appeal to _____ (man) and women across many _____ (culture).

9. Her stories often highlight the _____ (challenge) of cross-cultural living.

10. Amy Tan wrote her first book after meeting her _____ (half sister) in China.

11. In *The Joy Luck Club*, the author explores the different _____ (point of view) held by mothers and daughters.

12. *The Joy Luck Club* is divided into 16 _____ (chapter).

13. She has written many other _____ (book).

14. They also explore the relationships among mothers, daughters, and _____ (sister).

15. Amy Tan also plays in a band that raises money for various _____ (charity).

Write a sentence using the plural form of each noun.

16. radio, patio _____

17. dish, shelf _____

18. thief, roof _____

19. medium, video _____

20. goose, mouse _____

For additional help, review pages 4–5 in your textbook or visit www.voyagesinenglish.com.

1.3 Nouns as Subjects and Subject Complements

The **subject** tells what the sentence is about. A **subject complement** renames the subject; it refers to the same person, place, thing, or idea. A subject complement follows a linking verb.

Underline the subject of each sentence once. Underline each subject complement twice. Not all the sentences have subject complements.

1. My oldest brother is a pediatric doctor at County Hospital.
2. The wet newspaper lay at the end of the long, winding driveway.
3. The princess of that tiny country is a college student at the university.
4. Mrs. Green is my favorite math teacher at Seaside Middle School.
5. The fireworks lit up the night sky and filled the air with booms, whistles, and pops.
6. The campfire threw off sparks when John set another log on it.
7. Night crawlers are excellent bait for some freshwater fish, such as trout, carp, and walleye.
8. The seventh-grade class prepared for the trip to Washington, D.C.
9. The girls are members of the traveling soccer team.
10. The winners of the three-legged race were this pair of boys.
11. This former astronaut was also a professor at a nearby university.
12. The people in the newspaper story are heroes and should be recognized for their efforts.

Write whether each italicized noun is a *subject* or *subject complement*. Then underline the noun each subject complement renames.

13. Natalie's *necklace* is made of gold and silver. _____
14. The new rock band is *Seven Penguins.* _____
15. The tart apple was a crisp *surprise.* _____
16. A *raisin* was found on the windowsill. _____
17. This quaint *town* is Four Corners. _____

Write a subject complement to complete each sentence.

18. The bus is _____.
19. His movie was _____.
20. The music was _____.
21. Our class is _____.
22. Many students are _____.

For additional help, review pages 6–7 in your textbook or visit www.voyagesinenglish.com.

1.4 Nouns as Objects and Object Complements

The **direct object** tells *whom* or *what* after the verb. An **indirect object** tells *to whom* or *for whom*, or *to what* or *for what* the action is done. A noun can also be the **object of a preposition** or an **object complement.**

Write whether each italicized noun is a *direct object* or an *indirect object*.

1. I threw the *ball* for my dog. _____

2. She taught *Milo* after class on Wednesday. _____

3. We sang funny *songs* as we strolled the halls. _____

4. Hank gave the *postmaster* five dollars for postage. _____

5. Millie and Seymour baked a delicious *cake*. _____

6. Eva bought a *box* of chocolates for her aunt. _____

7. Josh sent his *uncle* a batch of brownies. _____

8. Dr. Hawkins stitched the *cut* on her finger. _____

9. The giraffe chewed the *leaves* on the tallest branches. _____

10. Our team yelled a *cheer* for Leon after his amazing catch. _____

Write a noun to complete each object of a preposition.

11. The embroidery on the _____ was done by _____.

12. The rain fell on the _____ and ruined it.

13. We will leave after the _____.

14. We sent a quart of soup to _____ in hopes it would help her get well.

15. We walked into _____ without any fear.

16. Several people travel over _____ during _____.

17. In _____, the leaves of _____ turn a variety of _____.

Write an object complement to rename each direct object.

18. The students elected Helena _____.

19. The team selected Josh _____.

20. The teachers announced the concert _____.

21. The entire group unanimously declared blue and gold _____.

22. Katrina and Josie chose flowers _____.

© Loyola Press. Voyages in English Grade 7

For additional help, review pages 8–9 in your textbook or visit www.voyagesinenglish.com.

1.4 Nouns as Objects and Object Complements

The **direct object** tells *whom* or *what* after the verb. An **indirect object** tells *to whom* or *for whom*, or *to what* or *for what* the action is done. A noun can also be the **object of a preposition** or an **object complement**.

Write whether each italicized noun is a *direct object*, an *indirect object*, an *object of a preposition*, or an *object complement*.

1. Music lovers consider Scott Joplin a popular *composer*. _____

2. Ragtime music started as African American dance *music*. _____

3. Eventually it became popular with the general *public*. _____

4. Ragtime played a *part* in the development of jazz. _____

5. Scott Joplin wrote and performed *ragtime*. _____

6. This music is a kind of march that depends on *syncopation*. _____

7. Syncopation highlights unexpected *beats*. _____

8. This rhythm gave the *music* the name "ragged time." _____

9. Later "ragged time" was shortened to *ragtime*. _____

10. Ragtime became less popular after Scott Joplin's *death*. _____

11. Many people declare Joplin's music a great *achievement*. _____

12. He remains the best-known ragtime figure in *history*. _____

13. Ragtime music is still popular among many piano *players*. _____

Write sentences using each of the following at least once: a direct object, an indirect object, an object of a preposition, and an object complement.

14. _____

_____

15. _____

_____

16. _____

_____

17. _____

_____

For additional help, review pages 8–9 in your textbook or visit www.voyagesinenglish.com.

1.5 Appositives

An **appositive** renames a noun. A **restrictive appositive** is necessary in order to understand the sentence. A **nonrestrictive appositive** is not necessary to understand the sentence and is set off with a comma or commas.

Circle the appositives. Then underline the noun each appositive explains.

1. Sheila, my cousin, works in that department store.

2. I love to visit Pine Acres, our cabin in the mountains.

3. Our neighbor Paul is away on vacation.

4. The black widow, a spider, is poisonous.

5. Mr. James, the principal, is in the cafeteria with his brother, the third-grade teacher.

6. Our dog Blue likes to climb up and sit in my lap.

7. My friend Bindi comes from India.

8. The Nile, a river, is located in Africa.

9. Albert Einstein, a physicist, revolutionized the study of space.

10. Springfield, the capital of Illinois, is my hometown.

11. The actor Katharine Hepburn has won more Oscars than any other actor.

12. Portland, the largest city in Oregon, is wet and rainy most of the year.

Write a sentence using each phrase in parentheses as an appositive to explain the italicized noun. Add commas as needed.

13. Grandma likes to play *mah jongg*. (a Chinese board game)

_____

14. *Pablo Picasso* was an influential figure in the visual arts. (the cofounder of cubism)

_____

15. *Charlie Chaplin* lived from 1889 to 1977. (the legendary actor)

_____

16. Irving Berlin wrote *"White Christmas."* (the best-selling song of all time)

_____

17. *Jim Thorpe* excelled in baseball, football, and track and field. (the great American athlete)

_____

For additional help, review pages 10–11 in your textbook or visit www.voyagesinenglish.com.

1.5 Appositives

An **appositive** renames a noun. A **restrictive appositive** is necessary in order to understand the sentence. A **nonrestrictive appositive** is not necessary to understand the sentence and is set off with a comma or commas.

Underline each appositive. Circle the noun it explains. Write *R* if the appositive is restrictive and *N* if it is nonrestrictive.

1. Jackie Robinson, the grandson of slaves, broke professional baseball's color barrier. _____

2. The Dodgers retired Robinson's number, 42, in 1972. _____

3. Branch Rickey was manager of a baseball team, the Brooklyn Dodgers. _____

4. The great right-hander Cy Young was a legendary baseball pitcher. _____

5. John learned the Boy Scout slogan, "Do a Good Turn Daily." _____

6. The famous songwriter Cole Porter was named after his mother's last name. _____

7. Chris loves to eat chorizo, a spicy sausage. _____

8. The American composer Aaron Copland meant to develop a uniquely American form of classical music. _____

9. The national poet Robert Frost recited one of his own works at the inauguration. _____

10. Ryan, my brother, loves to play hockey after school. _____

Use each set of words to write a sentence using an appositive.

11. Albert Einstein (genius)

_____

12. African American Olympic champion (Jesse Owens)

_____

13. Pennsylvania (the Keystone State)

_____

14. goal (to improve my soccer game)

_____

15. our sponsor (Ed's Tires and Brakes)

_____

For additional help, review pages 10–11 in your textbook or visit www.voyagesinenglish.com.

© Loyola Press. Voyages in English **Grade 7**

1.6 Possessive Nouns

A **possessive noun** expresses possession or ownership. To form the singular possessive, add -'s to the singular form of the noun, even if the noun ends in s. To form the possessive of plural nouns ending in s, add the apostrophe only.

Write the singular possessive and the plural possessive forms of each noun.

1. tomato   _____   _____

2. country   _____   _____

3. salmon   _____   _____

4. cliff   _____   _____

5. loaf   _____   _____

6. cross   _____   _____

7. key   _____   _____

8. attorney-at-law _____   _____

9. Chris   _____   _____

Underline each possessive noun. Write *S* if it is singular and *P* if it is plural.

10. The new radios were stacked neatly on Sandy's shelf.

11. The scientist crawled into the wolves' den to study their habits.

12. Eli's science project was very well prepared and deserved a high grade.

13. We went from Odette's house to Cayla's pool where I borrowed the twins' towel.

14. The plants' gorgeous coloring was nearly hidden by the thick grasses.

15. The Stevens's yard was covered by the old oak's autumn leaves.

16. The reindeer's hooves thundered as they passed over the tundra's frozen ground.

17. Mrs. Michael's dogs' bones were scattered among the pebbles in the tiny yard.

For additional help, review pages 12–13 in your textbook or visit www.voyagesinenglish.com.

1.6 Possessive Nouns

When nouns are used together to show **separate possession**, -'s is added to each noun. If the nouns show **joint possession**, -'s is added after the last noun.

Write _S_ if the sentence shows separate possession. Write _J_ if the sentence shows joint possession.

1. Kara and Anthony's paper was about the Great Depression. _____
2. Jake's and Jill's rattles are in the crib. _____
3. Men's and boys' pants are sold in that department. _____
4. My cousin and aunt's house is in Texas. _____
5. Lakesha and Chelsea's poster won the contest. _____
6. Mr. Clark's and Mrs. Williams's classrooms are next to each other. _____
7. The admiral's and the general's orders were given to the troops. _____
8. Lucky and Pretty Boy's birdcage is in the kitchen. _____

Rewrite each sentence to indicate separate possession.

9. Katrina and Josie projects were completed before Michael project.

_____

10. We will visit San Francisco and Oakland museums next spring.

_____

11. Do you think we can borrow Arif and Jaden bikes for the camping trip?

_____

12. I thought Rivu and Bryce paintings showed incredible talent.

_____

13. Chris and Paige dogs were barking all night and kept us awake.

_____

14. Tiko and Onose pencils are blue, but mine are yellow.

_____

15. The president and vice president goals were nearly identical on this issue.

_____

© Loyola Press. Voyages in English   Grade 7

For additional help, review pages 12–13 in your textbook or visit www.voyagesinenglish.com.

SECTION 2 Daily Maintenance

2.1 **The attorneys are presenting their arguments to the judge.**
1. What are the nouns in the sentence?   _____
2. Which noun is singular?   _____
3. What tense is the verb?   _____
4. What kind of word is *their?*   _____
5. Diagram the sentence here.

2.2 **His sister is the best singer in the choir.**
1. Which noun is the subject of the sentence?   _____
2. Which noun is the subject complement?   _____
3. What is the simple predicate in the sentence? _____
4. What kind of verb is it?   _____
5. Diagram the sentence here.

2.3 **The players chose Max captain of the football team.**
1. Which noun is a direct object?   _____
2. Which noun is an object complement?   _____
3. What is the prepositional phrase?   _____
4. What is the object of the preposition?   _____
5. Diagram the sentence here.

2.4 **My friend Nicole is an accomplished violinist.**
1. What is the appositive in the sentence? _____
2. What noun does it explain? _____
3. Is the appositive restrictive or nonrestrictive? _____
4. What part of speech is the word *an?* _____
5. Diagram the sentence here.

2.5 **The women's restroom is near the teachers' lounge.**
1. What are the possessive nouns in the sentence? _____
2. Are these nouns singular or plural? _____
3. Which word is a preposition? _____
4. What is the object of the preposition? _____
5. Diagram the sentence here.

© Loyola Press. Voyages in English **Grade 7**

2.1 Descriptive Adjectives, Position of Adjectives

A **descriptive adjective** gives information, such as color, number, or size, about a noun or pronoun. An adjective may come before a noun, directly follow a noun, act as a subject complement, or act as an object complement.

Underline the descriptive adjectives. Then circle the noun each adjective modifies.

1. Every wonderful vista gave me insight into why tourists choose to visit this area.

2. The quarrelsome children settled into a peaceful slumber.

3. Melanie is so calm and thoughtful.

4. I decided nine guests were more than enough after I calculated the cost of each meal.

5. The young man is exceptionally skillful with this difficult program.

Underline each adjective. Identify its position by writing *BN* if the adjective comes before the noun it describes, *AN* if it comes after the noun, *SC* if it is a subject complement, or *OC* if it is an object complement.

6. Elliot is talented and creative.   _____

7. The orange seed pod on that plant is delicate.   _____

8. The ripe tomato is just the size for a delicious salad.   _____

9. My brother found the golf tournament difficult.   _____

10. In the spring the lush green hills invite us all to go for a hike. _____

11. The persistent runner pushed through the crowd to the finish.   _____

12. Mr. Lee was short-tempered, but he was also fair.   _____

13. I really love taffy, chewy and sweet.   _____

Write a descriptive adjective to complete each sentence.

14. I decided to buy _____ _____ watermelons.

15. My favorite food is _____ and _____.

16. We all sat around the _____ table.

17. Tenicia dyed the fabric _____.

18. Kay writes _____ poetry and _____ short stories.

19. Every summer is too _____, and every winter is too _____.

20. The _____ _____ cat stalked the _____ mouse.

For additional help, review pages 18–19 in your textbook or visit www.voyagesinenglish.com.

2.2 Demonstrative, Interrogative, and Indefinite Adjectives

Demonstrative adjectives point out definite people, places, things, or ideas. **Interrogative adjectives** are used in questions. **Indefinite adjectives** refer to any or all of a group. Indefinite adjectives can be singular or plural.

Write whether each italicized adjective is *demonstrative*, *interrogative*, or *indefinite*.

1. *That* necklace belongs to Sophia. _____

2. *Some* boys brought home the wallets they made at camp. _____

3. *What* week are we going on vacation? _____

4. Have you made *this* meal before? _____

5. *Those* flowers grow well in the sun. _____

6. *Whose* laundry is in the washing machine? _____

Underline the demonstrative, interrogative, or indefinite adjectives.

7. Which dessert did you choose?

8. Every child can submit a single entry into this contest.

9. We saw several kinds of kitchen wallpaper, but I liked only a few designs.

10. I know you didn't get these shoes at this store, so which store had them?

11. That teacher told us to choose any desk.

12. Mom asked, "Will you bring me another plate from that stack on the counter?"

Complete each sentence with a demonstrative, an interrogative, or an indefinite adjective.

13. Every _____ days Kyle would ask his mother if he could get a dog.

14. Diego decided to invite _____ of his friends over to play games on his birthday.

15. The police determined that _____ driver was responsible for the accident.

16. Mrs. Holbert decided that we needed _____ day to complete the assignment.

17. _____ set of collectors' cards has Vlad acquired _____ week?

18. I don't know _____ decision to make about _____ problem.

19. _____ lockers still need to be cleaned out for the summer.

20. Will you bring me _____ new notebooks?

For additional help, review pages 20–21 in your textbook or visit www.voyagesinenglish.com.

© Loyola Press. Voyages in English Grade 7

3.5 **Several students in Ms. Ling's dance class entered the talent show.**
1. Which word is an indefinite adjective?   _____
2. Is this word singular or plural?   _____
3. What are the other adjectives in the sentence?   _____
4. Which word is used as a preposition?   _____
5. Diagram the sentence on another sheet of paper.

3.6 **Which player is the tallest one on the volleyball team?**
1. Which word is an interrogative adjective?   _____
2. What kind of adjective is the word *tallest?*   _____
3. Which noun is used as a subject complement?   _____
4. Which noun is the object of a preposition?   _____
5. Diagram the sentence on another sheet of paper.

3.7 **Jim's and Bob's robots are good, but mine is better.**
1. What are the adjectives in the sentence?   _____
2. Which word is a comparative adjective?   _____
3. Which nouns show possession?   _____
4. Do they show separate or joint possession?   _____
5. Diagram the sentence on another sheet of paper.

3.8 **Her report on global warming was very informative.**
1. What is the compound noun in the sentence?   _____
2. What does the adjective phrase modify?   _____
3. What is the adjective *informative* used as?   _____
4. What part of speech is the word *very?*   _____
5. Diagram the sentence on another sheet of paper.

3.9 **This bedroom has less space than that bedroom.**
1. What are the demonstrative adjectives? _____
2. Which word is used as a comparative adjective? _____
3. Which word does this adjective modify? _____
4. What kind of noun does this adjective compare? _____
5. Diagram the sentence on another sheet of paper.

3.10 **Each job applicant must submit these forms.**
1. What kind of word is *Each?* _____
2. Is this word singular or plural? _____
3. What kind of word is *these?* _____
4. Is this word singular or plural? _____
5. Diagram the sentence on another sheet of paper.

3.11 **The proud parents applauded their children's achievements.**
1. Which word is used as a descriptive adjective? _____
2. Which word is a possessive noun? _____
3. Is this word singular or plural? _____
4. Which word is a possessive adjective? _____
5. Diagram the sentence on another sheet of paper.

3.1 Person, Number, and Gender of Pronouns

A **pronoun** is a word used in place of a noun. The word that a pronoun refers to is called its **antecedent.** Pronouns change form depending on **person, number,** or **gender.**

Write the person and number of each italicized pronoun.

1. *They* went to the new water park.   _____

2. After lunch the tickets were divided among *us*.   _____

3. It must have been *she* who bought the card.   _____

4. *You* should wear this pair of sneakers.   _____

5. Beth gave *me* a lecture about cleaning up the kitchen. _____

6. *We* do not want to wake up late tomorrow.   _____

Circle the pronouns. Write *1* above each first-person pronoun, *2* above each second-person pronoun, and *3* above each third-person pronoun.

7. Have you heard of the great ballplayer Joe DiMaggio? Many people say he was one of the

   best players in baseball history. They point to that stellar ball-playing record attributed to

   him. But Joltin' Joe, as he was called, also had a sense of grace and privacy about him.

   He was married to actress Marilyn Monroe, and I wouldn't think that marriage could have

   survived such a need for privacy. But you might be interested to know that after she died,

   he sent roses to that grave site for 20 years. I think he really loved her.

Use the directions in parentheses to finish each sentence with the correct pronoun.

8. He is going to the shelter with _____ tomorrow afternoon. (first person singular)

9. _____ got the idea from a friend who lives there. (first person plural)

10. _____ says there are lots of families living at the shelter. (third person singular)

11. Parents need babysitters so _____ can go out for awhile. (third person plural)

12. We'll play games with the kids, and _____ will have fun. (third person plural)

13. We would like _____ to come too. (second person singular)

14. You could ride with _____ to the shelter. (first person plural)

15. If _____ goes well, we hope to go back next week too. (third person singular)

© Loyola Press. Voyages in English   **Grade 7**

For additional help, review pages 32–33 in your textbook or visit www.voyagesinenglish.com.

Section 3 • 25

3.2 Subject Pronouns

A **subject pronoun** can be the subject or subject complement of a sentence. The subject pronouns are *I*, *we*, *you*, *he*, *she*, *it*, and *they*.

Circle the correct pronoun to complete each sentence. Then write *subject* or *subject complement* to indicate how the pronoun is used.

1. Kenny and (I   me) will write the report together. _____
2. Is it (him   he) at the gate? _____
3. Was it (she   her) who went to London? _____
4. Tomorrow Juan and (they   them) will go swimming. _____
5. It was (he   him) who took the notebook. _____
6. Ty thought it was Joy and (her   she) who went running. _____
7. The person who climbed the hill was (me   I). _____
8. (Me   I) went looking for butterflies. _____
9. (They   Them) took Carmen to the train station. _____
10. Was it (he   him) who caught the largest fish? _____

Complete each sentence with a subject pronoun that matches its underlined antecedent.

11. My <u>brother and I</u> play trumpets, and _____ are both in the school band.
12. The <u>Harrison twins</u> play French horns, so _____ are in the band too.
13. Their <u>father</u> is the band director, and we all think _____ is pretty cool.
14. Our <u>mother</u> never misses a concert, and _____ always says we played well.
15. One day my <u>brother</u> broke my trumpet when _____ dropped it.
16. My parents took the <u>instrument</u> to the music store where _____ was fixed.

Write five sentences that describe a family member you admire. Use personal pronouns as the subjects and subject complements.

17. _____
18. _____
19. _____
20. _____
21. _____

© Loyola Press. Voyages in English   Grade 7

For additional help, review pages 34–35 in your textbook or visit www.voyagesinenglish.com.

3.3 Object Pronouns

An **object pronoun** can be used as the object of a verb or a preposition.
The object pronouns are *me*, *us*, *you*, *him*, *her*, *it*, and *them*.

Underline each personal pronoun. Write *D* if it is a direct object, *I* if it is an indirect object, or *O* if it is an object of a preposition.

1. Val told me the whole story on Monday afternoon. _____

2. The senator from Alaska greeted them on the tour of the Capitol. _____

3. Carlos and Miguel saw her at the library downtown. _____

4. Pat heard that there is an expert on pioneer life among us. _____

5. Samuel could not believe that Mr. Lopez loaned him the pliers. _____

6. Can Teresa stand between Jane and me? _____

7. Even the most familiar teachers did not recognize you in disguise. _____

8. Peter spoke fluent Italian with them. _____

Write the correct pronoun to complete each sentence.

9. I hoped the coach would pick _____ to demonstrate the kick. (I   me)

10. I did not ask why he needed the pencil; I just gave it to _____. (him   he)

11. My dad is going camping with _____ next weekend. (we   us)

12. Paulina gave the box to _____ after the piano recital. (she   her)

13. All of _____ decided to get the teacher a present. (we   us)

14. We saw _____ at the movie theater downtown. (them   they)

15. Armando gave the bike to June and _____. (I   me)

Write the pronoun that correctly replaces the italicized antecedent.

16. Natalie went grocery shopping with each of *her brothers*. _____

17. My grandmother wants to see *my mom, my dad, my brother, and me*. _____

18. Our neighbor offered *Ava* money to mow the grass and trim the hedges. _____

19. The music teacher is married to *Coach Stevens*. _____

20. Carla sang *the song* as loudly as she could so everyone could hear. _____

21. To win the softball game was the goal of Carol and *Sheila*. _____

22. We liked Rover immediately and talked Mom into keeping *the dog*. _____

23. Yesterday my math teacher called *my parents*. _____

For additional help, review pages 36–37 in your textbook
or visit www.voyagesinenglish.com.

3.4 Pronouns After *Than* or *As*

The words *than* and *as* are used in comparisons. These **conjunctions** join two clauses, but remember that sometimes part of the second clause is omitted.

Circle the correct pronoun to complete each sentence. Then write the verb that has been omitted from the second clause.

1. Little Billy cries more than (he   him).   _____

2. Marie sings better than (she   her).   _____

3. Craig dances as well as (they   them).   _____

4. Does Brenda practice as much as (he   him)?   _____

5. Jamal ordered more food than (I   me).   _____

6. The children were joyous, and the adults were as happy as (they   them).   _____

7. Samuel was more startled by the fireworks than (she   her). _____

8. Willis plays piano better than (he   him).   _____

9. Aisha ate more hot dogs than (I   me).   _____

10. Chuck took more time to finish than (I   me).   _____

Use the chart to write sentences with *than* or *as* followed by pronouns.

	KEVIN	KATYA	MARIA
Games Won	5	5	7
Games Lost	2	3	0

11. Compared with Kevin:

_____

_____

12. Compared with Katya:

_____

_____

13. Compared with Maria:

_____

_____

For additional help, review pages 38–39 in your textbook or visit www.voyagesinenglish.com.

© Loyola Press. Voyages in English **Grade 7**

3.5 Possessive Pronouns and Adjectives

Possessive pronouns show possession or ownership. The possessive pronouns are *mine, ours, yours, his, hers, its,* and *theirs.* The **possessive adjectives** are *my, our, your, his, her, its,* and *their;* they always precede nouns.

Underline the possessive pronoun or the possessive adjective in each sentence. Circle the noun each possessive adjective modifies.

1. I would like to have an outfit like hers.
2. His shirt is the one with the striped pattern.
3. Mine is the house with the blue shutters.
4. I hope our skit is chosen for the school assembly.
5. You left your backpack in the gymnasium.
6. The black-and-white cat is theirs.
7. May I collect yours?

Complete each sentence with a possessive adjective. Use context clues.

8. The jacket is mine. I gave her _____ jacket because she looked so cold.
9. The house is theirs. We went to _____ house for lunch.
10. The collar belongs to the dog. Fido just loves _____ collar.
11. Layla made a dress. We all want one just like _____ dress.
12. Jacob built a table. He gave _____ table to the school for its charity auction.
13. Willem has five cards. He gave three of _____ cards to Tess.
14. Louis and Jaden did a great job. We think _____ project was the best.
15. Alaina won first place. Did you see _____ trophy?

Write a possessive that can replace the italicized words. Then write *A* if the word is a possessive adjective or *P* if it is a possessive pronoun.

16. The bikes are *my family's and mine.* _____ _____
17. I think the dog is locked in *Collin's* room. _____ _____
18. Mom is cooking so she won't let us in *Mom's* kitchen. _____ _____
19. Don't throw away the old blankets; they are *my blankets.* _____ _____
20. David took those photos in college. They are *David's photos.* _____ _____
21. The red-and-white ball is *Destiny and Eli's ball.* _____ _____
22. *Josef's* bag is the one lying in the hall. _____ _____

For additional help, review pages 40–41 in your textbook or visit www.voyagesinenglish.com.

3.6 Intensive and Reflexive Pronouns

An **intensive pronoun** is used to emphasize a preceding noun or pronoun.
A **reflexive pronoun** is used as the direct or indirect object of a verb or the object of a preposition.

Underline the intensive or reflexive pronoun in each sentence. Write whether the pronoun is *intensive* or *reflexive*.

1. You yourself must make this difficult decision. _____
2. We taught ourselves the song they sing at all the football games. _____
3. I myself liked the idea, but it did not pass at the meeting. _____
4. Can you really do all that work yourselves? _____
5. Enrico himself ran to the store for butter. _____
6. Kay laughed at herself and decided to give it another try. _____
7. I decided to take myself to the movies. _____
8. We ourselves preferred the pumpkin pie over the pecan pie. _____
9. You deserve to congratulate yourselves on a job well done. _____
10. Quinn caught himself starting to yawn again and stifled it quickly. _____

Complete each sentence with an intensive or a reflexive pronoun. Then write *I* if the pronoun is intensive or *R* if it is reflexive.

11. We _____ thought we would win the game. _____
12. You all must prepare _____ for the test. _____
13. You _____ should try it. _____
14. I will finish the project _____. _____
15. Dennis excused _____ from the room. _____
16. The campers found _____ in a bad storm. _____
17. Kate taught _____ to crochet a scarf. _____
18. The dog _____ will star in a movie. _____
19. Jack decided to write a song for the school _____. _____

On another sheet of paper, write about a time when, as a child, you attempted a difficult task on your own. Use at least three intensive or reflexive pronouns. Circle each intensive pronoun. Underline each reflexive pronoun.

For additional help, review pages 42–43 in your textbook or visit www.voyagesinenglish.com.

3.7 Agreement of Pronouns and Antecedents

Pronouns must agree with their **antecedents** in person, number, and gender.

Underline the antecedent for each italicized pronoun.

1. Julius Robert Oppenheimer did not use *his* first name.
2. Oppenheimer led the scientists of the Manhattan Project. *They* developed the atomic bomb.
3. Robert Oppenheimer was a theoretical physicist, and *he* taught physics.
4. He *himself* came from a wealthy family of businessmen and artists.
5. Robert Oppenheimer was brilliant. *He* spoke eight languages.
6. When Oppenheimer needed to present a lecture in Dutch, he learned *it* in only six weeks.
7. The U.S. government established the Manhattan Project in 1941. *It* put Oppenheimer in charge one year later.
8. The scientists successfully tested the first atomic bomb on July 16, 1945. Oppenheimer said, "*We* knew the world would not be the same."
9. Less than a month later, U.S. planes dropped two bombs on cities in Japan. *They* killed more than 140,000 people.
10. The bombs ended World War II, but Oppenheimer said, "The physicists have known sin; and this is a knowledge which *they* cannot lose."

Write the pronoun that goes with each underlined antecedent.

11. Oppenheimer had a brother, <u>Frank</u>, who was a physicist himself. _____
12. His wife was <u>Katherine Oppenheimer</u>. She was known as Kitty. _____
13. Their daughter was <u>Toni</u>. She was born during the Manhattan Project. _____
14. Their son was <u>Peter</u>. He was their firstborn child. _____
15. <u>Oppenheimer</u> himself upset many powerful men of the time. _____
16. The <u>men</u> agreed among themselves that he was no longer helpful. _____
17. All had security clearance, but <u>Oppenheimer</u> was stripped of his. _____
18. But in 1963 the <u>U.S. president</u> himself gave Oppenheimer a prize. _____
19. The <u>prize</u> honored the man, and he clearly valued it. _____

On another sheet of paper, write three sentences that each have a clear antecedent and a related pronoun.

For additional help, review pages 44–45 in your textbook or visit www.voyagesinenglish.com.

© Loyola Press. Voyages in English Grade 7

Section 3 • 31

3.7 Agreement of Pronouns and Antecedents

Pronouns must agree with their **antecedents** in person, number, and gender.

Underline the antecedent of each italicized pronoun. Write its person (1, 2, or 3), its number (S or P), and, if it applies, its gender (F, M, or N).

1. _____ Chess is a game of strategy. *It* does not take long to learn, but it can take a lifetime to master.

2. _____ Are you going to play the trivia game John brought? I like to play with *him* because he is fair.

3. _____ Players today can choose from many different kinds of games. *They* can choose from very high-tech games to simple word games.

4. _____ My friend Amy has a toy with far more ancient roots. *She* loves her game of mancala.

5. _____ My brother and I like to play a game in the car. Every time *we* see a certain kind of car, we yell "Bug!"

6. _____ Ann and Ron, have *you* ever played with jacks? It takes some concentration.

7. _____ A jump rope is good exercise, too, but *it* requires good coordination.

8. _____ John and Raul are playing with puzzle cubes. *They* are tricky to solve.

Complete each sentence with an appropriate pronoun. Make sure that each agrees in person, number, and gender with its antecedent. Underline the antecedent.

9. Will you and I be partners on the field trip? If so, _____ can talk then.

10. Maggie and Paige have invited their mothers to come along with _____.

11. Grandma adopts homeless animals, and five now live with _____.

12. Mr. Barton gave us the key. After we lock up, we need to take it back to _____.

13. Tenecia is a champion gymnast. We are going to watch _____ compete today.

14. Where are Rivu and Walter? I have been looking everywhere for _____.

15. Have Andy and Ayanna called? _____ were going to call me this afternoon.

16. Do not jump on the couch, because _____ might collapse.

17. Have you seen Thomas? This book belongs to _____.

18. If you see Bryona, tell _____ that Christy and Erica are looking for the book.

19. Max and I are leaving soon, and you can arrive with _____.

On another sheet of paper, write three sentences that include clear antecedents and their related pronouns.

For additional help, review pages 44–45 in your textbook or visit www.voyagesinenglish.com.

4.1 Principal Parts of Verbs

The three **principal parts** of a verb are the **base form,** the **past,** and the **past participle.** The **present participle** is made by adding -*ing* to the base form. A **verb phrase** is two or more verbs that work together as a unit.

Underline each verb or verb phrase. Circle the auxiliary verb in each verb phrase.

1. We have chosen blue and yellow for the team's colors.

2. Henry and Vlad fixed Michael's bicycle this morning.

3. Dana, Katya, and Timothy flew to Texas last week.

4. I had called her yesterday, but she did not answer.

5. Neal and Abigail could hear the sound of rain on the tin roof of the front porch.

6. My sister and her husband drove me home tonight after play rehearsal.

Write the base, past, and past participle forms for each verb that you underlined in the sentences above.

BASE	PAST	PAST PARTICIPLE
7. _____	_____	_____
8. _____	_____	_____
9. _____	_____	_____
10. _____	_____	_____
11. _____	_____	_____
12. _____	_____	_____
13. _____	_____	_____

Complete each sentence with the past or past participle form of the verb in parentheses.

14. We _____ (give) the bell ringer two dollars for the charity.

15. Constance _____ (sing) beautifully at the service last week.

16. Hope and Kaylee _____ (work) on the assignment all day Saturday.

17. Did you know that plastic was _____ (develop) over a hundred years ago?

18. My dog was _____ (pick) to be on the fly ball team this year.

19. The neighbors have _____ (go) on vacation to Morocco this winter.

20. Chris and John have _____ (eat) their breakfast already.

For additional help, review pages 58–59 in your textbook or visit www.voyagesinenglish.com.

4.2   Transitive and Intransitive Verbs

A **transitive verb** expresses an action that passes from a doer to a receiver.
A **phrasal verb** is a combination of the main verb and a preposition or an adverb.
An **intransitive verb** does not have a receiver for its action.

**Underline the verb, verb phrase, or phrasal verb in each sentence.
Write whether it is transitive (*T*) or intransitive (*I*). If it is transitive,
circle the direct object.**

1. Aesop made up fables,short moral stories with mostly animals as characters.   _____

2. The moral messages within these fables remain relevant today.   _____

3. One famous Aesop fable is called "The Fox and the Stork."   _____

4. One day Stork ran into Fox.   _____

5. Fox invited Stork to his home for dinner.   _____

6. Fox served soup in a large, wide bowl.   _____

7. With her long beak, Stork could not sip the soup.   _____

8. Stork left with a hungry belly.   _____

9. A few days later, Fox came to Stork's house for dinner.   _____

10. Fox found little pieces of food at the bottom of a jar with a long, narrow neck.   _____

11. Stork's long beak fit easily.   _____

12. Fox's nose did not fit in the jar.   _____

13. Stork just shrugged her shoulders.   _____

14. After all, she had learned from Fox.   _____

**Write two sentences for each verb. Use it as a transitive verb in the first
sentence and as an intransitive verb in the second sentence.**

15. **drive**

   Transitive: _____

   Intransitive: _____

16. **teach**

   Transitive: _____

   Intransitive: _____

17. **help**

   Transitive: _____

   Intransitive: _____

For additional help, review pages 60–61 in your textbook
or visit www.voyagesinenglish.com.

© Loyola Press. Voyages in English   **Grade 7**

4.2 Transitive and Intransitive Verbs

A **transitive verb** expresses an action that passes from a doer to a receiver.
A **phrasal verb** is a combination of the main verb and a preposition or an adverb.
An **intransitive verb** does not have a receiver for its action.

Underline the transitive verbs. Circle the intransitive verbs.

1. The lifeguards gave safety lessons by the pool.

2. The little puppy shivered and then shook in the rain and snow.

3. John coughed loudly, but we all ignored him.

4. Every day at the lake, it rained or snowed.

5. Ken and James threw the ball for the dog.

6. Allison studied long into the night and aced her spelling exam.

7. The cats pounce and the kittens leap over each other at my house.

8. The Hendersons' lush garden produces buckets of ripe vegetables every summer.

9. My younger brother sets up Civil War figurines and then reenacts epic battles.

10. I can concentrate only when I study at the library or in my room.

**Underline the transitive verbs and circle the intransitive verbs.
Then complete each sentence with an appropriate transitive or
intransitive verb.**

11. The child closed his eyes and _____ as he extinguished the candles.

12. Jorge usually walks, but today he _____ in his father's new red car.

13. Please tell me, did you _____ the new movie this weekend?

14. Grandma Ethel _____ and hugs us every time she visits.

15. Tina _____ the dust out of her eyes, so she avoided a scratch to her cornea.

16. I _____ the decrepit car as it backfired from three blocks away.

17. Ralph trembles because he will _____ from the 10-meter platform.

18. John _____ the song confidently because he knew all the words.

19. Uncle Albert always _____, and he sleeps well a result.

20. She _____, and the dogs ran to her immediately.

**On another sheet of paper, write about some typical things you and your
family do over a weekend. Then underline the transitive verbs and circle the
intransitive verbs you used.**

For additional help, review pages 60–61 in your textbook
or visit www.voyagesinenglish.com.

Section 4 • 43

© Loyola Press. Voyages in English   Grade 7

4.3 Troublesome Verbs

Troublesome verbs are those with similar pronunciations and spellings, but with different meanings and usage. These verb pairs are often confused.

Circle the verbs that correctly complete the sentences.

1. He (lied   laid) the wood in the fireplace.
2. I think I will (sit   set) here and rest for a while.
3. Please (let   leave) your shoes by the door.
4. You can (set   sit) that glass over there on the counter.
5. The sun (rose   raised) at 6:30 this morning.
6. The waves (raised   rose) above the dock during the storm.
7. (Let   Leave) Satsu sit by the window.
8. Please do not (rise   raise) your hands from the handlebars.
9. We watched the steam (raise   rise) from the cup of coffee.
10. The dog decided to (lay   lie) on the cold tile floor.
11. Did you (lend   borrow) that rake from Mr. McCoy?
12. We like to (lie   lay) on the sandy beach and soak up the summer sun.
13. The cat (sat   set) on the windowsill and cleaned herself meticulously in the moonlight.
14. Mr. Hawthorne (learned   taught) me the proper way to (rise   raise) the flag.
15. (Let   Leave) the video game alone, and please (sit   set) down at the table.
16. The gray striped cat (lay   laid) in the sun all afternoon.
17. Will you (sit   set) the bowl on the table and help me (raise   rise) the window?
18. My parents (let   leave) me go to the community center, but when I am ready to (let   leave), they will pick me up.
19. We should (lend   borrow) Amy our extra jacket.
20. Joe and I (learned   taught) how to tie knots and (sit   set) tent pegs last weekend.

Rewrite the sentences to correct the use of troublesome verbs.

21. Natalie learned me how to do the algebra problems with which I was struggling.

_____

22. Go set on the couch and rise your feet.

_____

23. Please don't let your clothes laying all over the house.

_____

24. May Herb and Jake lend our lawn mower and return it tomorrow?

_____

© Loyola Press. Voyages in English   **Grade 7**

For additional help, review pages 62–63 in your textbook or visit www.voyagesinenglish.com.

4.4 Linking Verbs

A **linking verb** does not express action. Instead, it joins a subject with a subject complement.

Complete each sentence with the part of speech in parentheses. Underline the linking verb.

1. The weather turned _____ last night. (adjective)

2. These sunflowers grow _____ in the garden. (adjective)

3. That person is an _____. (noun)

4. Although tired, the cat remained _____. (adjective)

5. Hector and Jayden are _____. (noun)

6. The fluffy buttermilk pancakes tasted _____. (adjective)

7. The water remained _____ even after the storm. (adjective)

8. The caterpillar became a _____. (noun)

Underline the linking verb in each sentence. Then write the subject complement for the linking verb.

9. The wasps became more active during the day. _____

10. Michael Jordan was an amazing basketball player. _____

11. Plymouth Drive was the street you should have taken. _____

12. The muffins from the bake sale tasted superb. _____

13. The winning players seem terribly nervous. _____

14. The referee remained calm throughout the game. _____

15. In the fairy tale, the lizard is actually a prince. _____

16. Lindsey feels excited about her tryout. _____

Underline the verb in each sentence. Then write whether that verb is transitive (*T*), intransitive (*I*), or linking (*L*).

17. Our family owns a set of dirt bikes. _____

18. My dad taught us the rules of the sport long ago. _____

19. My dirt bike is green with yellow flames. _____

20. Just about every weekend, we race in the desert. _____

21. My older sister is the best rider of us all. _____

For additional help, review pages 64–65 in your textbook
or visit www.voyagesinenglish.com.

4.5 Active and Passive Voices

When a verb is in the **active voice,** the subject is the doer of the action. In the **passive voice,** the subject is the receiver of the action.

Underline the verb or verb phrase in each sentence. Then write whether that verb is in the active voice (*A*) or passive voice (*P*).

1. The overripe fruit hit the ground with a splat.   _____
2. The story is read by the famous actor Melvin Belleville.   _____
3. My brother reads quietly in the green chair every evening.   _____
4. The bountiful harvest rewarded us all.   _____
5. Only the cars were damaged in the three-car accident.   _____
6. The stockings were hung by the youngest child in the family.   _____
7. All night the watchdog carefully guarded the front gate.   _____
8. The fire in the wood-burning stove is lit by me.   _____
9. The dutiful mother cat follows her young kittens around the house.   _____
10. Seventeen students participated in the trip to Washington, D.C.   _____

Rewrite each sentence by changing the verb from passive to active voice.

11. The trunk was lifted onto the bed by Charlie.

_____

12. The memo had been initialed by the chairperson.

_____

13. A new ambassador was nominated by the president.

_____

14. The dough will be kneaded by Ryan in the morning.

_____

15. The team was invited to the awards banquet by Coach Evans.

_____

16. The address numbers were nailed to the wall by a carpenter.

_____

17. The items on the rack were neatly organized by the sales associate.

_____

For additional help, review pages 66–67 in your textbook or visit www.voyagesinenglish.com.

4.6 Simple, Progressive, and Perfect Tenses

Simple tenses reflect the present, past, and future. **Progressive tenses** use a form of the auxiliary verb *be* and the main verb's present participle. **Perfect tenses** use a form of the auxiliary verb *have* and the main verb's past participle.

Underline each verb or verb phrase. Then write the letter that identifies its tense.

a. Simple tense   **b.** Progressive tense   **c.** Perfect tense

1. The tour bus will arrive at two o'clock this afternoon.   _____
2. The icicles melt in the warm sun.   _____
3. Her phone has been ringing all morning.   _____
4. Kyle is learning about the history of France.   _____
5. The pool will be opening the first week of June.   _____
6. Martin's fate had been decided in April.   _____
7. Sharon rode the roller coaster three times.   _____
8. The costumes will have been constructed by opening night.   _____
9. Jeremy was hiking on the Blue Mountain Trail.   _____
10. I have been finished with the test for a long time.   _____
11. Isaiah will apply to six schools in the area.   _____
12. This dog has been trained in only six weeks.   _____
13. The instructor will be giving each of us a schedule.   _____

Complete each sentence using the verb and tense in parentheses.

14. Holly and Emma _____. (*sing*—future progressive)

_____

15. My friends and I _____. (*offer*—past perfect active)

_____

16. The plants in the kitchen _____. (*water*—future perfect passive)

_____

17. Amanda's father _____. (*know*—present perfect)

_____

4.7 Indicative, Imperative, and Emphatic Moods

The **indicative mood** is used to state a fact or ask a question. The **imperative mood** is used to give commands. The **emphatic mood** gives emphasis to a simple present tense or past tense verb.

Underline the verb or verb phrase in each sentence. Then write whether the mood is *indicative*, *imperative*, or *emphatic*.

1. I can find the information for you.   _____

2. Kate, hold your sister's hand.   _____

3. When was Ronald Reagan president?   _____

4. I did clean my room this morning.   _____

5. You should use more salt in that recipe.   _____

6. Close the kitchen window.   _____

7. Please do not tap your foot, Jack.   _____

8. Juliet does love Romeo from the very first moment.   _____

9. He will read the new book to the children.   _____

10. Emily did run for class president.   _____

Rewrite each sentence in the imperative mood.

11. It is very important to read all the instructions before you build the birdhouse.

_____

12. The workers must be sure-footed and safety conscious.

_____

Rewrite each sentence in the indicative mood.

13. Learn to dance with rhythm and grace.

_____

14. Let's go to the beach today.

_____

Write a sentence in the emphatic mood.

15. _____

© Loyola Press. Voyages in English   **Grade 7**

For additional help, review pages 70–71 in your textbook or visit www.voyagesinenglish.com.

5.1   Participles

> **Verbals** are words made from verbs to function as another part of speech. A **participle** is a verb form used as an adjective. A **participial phrase** includes the participle, an object or a complement, and any modifiers.

Underline the participle in each sentence. Circle the noun or pronoun the participle modifies. Then underline the main verb twice.

1. Having eaten dinner, Colonel Mansard walked leisurely to the study.
2. He, entering the study, discovered that the silver had been stolen.
3. Did Mrs. Blaine, known for her extravagant lifestyle, take the silver?
4. Mr. Green, stalling for time, suggested everyone sit down for dinner.
5. Humming to herself, Abby seemed unconcerned by any of the fuss.
6. Professor Davis, having arrived late, was flustered by the events.
7. Mrs. Farin was cleared when the written confession matched her alibi completely.
8. A letter copied by hand implicated Mrs. Blaine and her ample handbag.

Underline the participial phrase in each sentence. Circle the noun or pronoun it modifies.

9. Having found the missing homework, Luis was relieved.
10. Workers cut down the trees burned in the wildfires.
11. The man speaking to the teacher is my father.
12. The signs posted on the wall are for next week's election.
13. A cat, wearing a blue collar, followed me home.
14. Can you reach the books placed on the top shelf?
15. The soup, boiling in the black pot, splattered all over the ceiling.
16. My favorite contestant was the dog taught to bark "Happy Birthday to You."
17. The hot tea, steaming in the blue mug, was a welcome sight on a cold day.
18. That silk dress hanging at the top of the display is finally on sale.

On another sheet of paper, write a sentence for each participial phrase. Circle the noun or pronoun that each participial phrase describes.

19. looking through her purse
20. holding the roll of tickets
21. wounded by the enemy
22. formed by stones and boulders
23. followed closely by the excited puppy
24. acknowledging their hard work

© Loyola Press. Voyages in English   Grade 7

For additional help, review pages 84–85 in your textbook or visit www.voyagesinenglish.com.

5.2 Placement of Participles

Do not confuse a **participial adjective** after a linking verb with a participle that is part of a verb phrase. **Dangling participles** occur when a sentence does not contain the noun or pronoun the participle modifies.

Underline the participial adjectives in these sentences.

1. We visited the bustling zoo over the holiday.

2. The pacing lion was popular with everyone.

3. A frazzled father was too busy chasing his young twin sons to see the polar bears.

4. The sleeping koalas were not disturbed by the screaming monkeys.

5. Everyone cheered when the elephants emerged from the darkened cave.

6. We noticed there were no buzzing insects near the bat exhibit.

7. The annoyed camel kept turning its back on the crowd.

8. The patient snake docent helped turn a frightened child into a smiling one.

9. We never leave the zoo without a glimpse of the flying squirrels.

10. This time we made sure to visit the traveling butterfly exhibit.

Write phrases using each participle as an adjective before a noun.

11. scrubbed _____

12. screaming _____

13. driven _____

14. broken _____

15. wasting _____

16. wounded _____

Rewrite each sentence to correct the dangling participle. Add words as needed.

17. Coming home early, the house was empty.

_____

18. Running through the park, a thunderous cheer erupted from the baseball field.

_____

19. Studying the footprints, it was the reason for the missing money.

_____

20. Examining the damage, the book should be replaced.

_____

For additional help, review pages 86–87 in your textbook or visit www.voyagesinenglish.com.

5.3 Gerunds as Subjects and Subject Complements

A **gerund** is a verb form ending in *-ing* that is used as a noun. The entire **gerund phrase**—made up of a gerund and any other parts—acts as a noun. A gerund can be used in a sentence as a subject or a subject complement.

Underline the gerund phrase in each sentence. Write *S* if the gerund is the subject or *SC* if the gerund is the subject complement.

1. Throwing footballs is the best way for a quarterback to practice.   _____

2. Jim's specialty is painting with oils.   _____

3. Putting together puzzles helped quiet the young child.   _____

4. Watching sports is one way that my brother passes his time.   _____

5. The girl's favorite pastime is listening to music.   _____

6. The high point of my trip was searching in the caves.   _____

7. Collecting stamps was how I received my last merit badge.   _____

8. Humming a familiar song helped the nervous actor stay calm.   _____

9. My least favorite job is vacuuming the hallway.   _____

10. Meena's preferred exercise is jogging through her neighborhood.   _____

Write a gerund used as a subject or a subject complement to complete each sentence.

11. _____ scientists to ask questions is what Jupiter does best.

12. An important part of the Juno project is _____ us understand the planets.

13. Juno's mission is _____ the largest gaseous planet in our solar system.

14. _____ into the swirling gases is a function of the spacecraft.

15. _____ difficult questions has long been the goal of our space programs.

16. _____ distant planets has captured the imagination of humanity.

17. Our major goal is _____ all these facts about space exploration.

Write a gerund phrase to complete each sentence. Use the verb in parentheses.

18. _____ was a great time. (visit)

19. _____ should be fun. (swim)

20. My aerobic exercise is _____. (run)

For additional help, review pages 88–89 in your textbook or visit www.voyagesinenglish.com.

5.4 Gerunds as Objects and Appositives

A gerund can be used as a direct object or as the object of a preposition. It can also be used as an appositive—a word or group of words used immediately after a noun to rename it and give more information about it.

Underline the gerund phrase in each sentence. Write whether the gerund is a direct object (*D*), an object of a preposition (*P*), or an appositive (*A*).

1. My grandmother enjoys cutting hair. _____
2. Malaya excels in baking bread. _____
3. Calligraphy, writing fancy letters, looks like an interesting hobby. _____
4. Her record of jumping rope is an amazing feat. _____
5. Jared's job, washing the car, is something he likes to do. _____
6. Almost immediately, Sarah regretted losing her purse. _____
7. Maya's new baby loves playing the peekaboo game. _____
8. We will celebrate all patriotic holidays by raising the flag. _____
9. The officer pulled the car over and avoided stopping traffic. _____
10. Ava's science project, making a volcano, took almost two hours. _____
11. With hard work the boys succeeded in raising their grades. _____
12. This recipe calls for kneading the dough for 10 minutes. _____
13. Some college students need more paper for taking notes. _____
14. Her schedule included visiting relatives. _____
15. This task, raking the fallen leaves, takes the most time. _____

Write a gerund phrase to complete each sentence. Write whether the gerund is a direct object (*D*), an object of a preposition (*P*), or an appositive (*A*).

16. I dread _____ because he scares me. _____
17. Cats and dogs benefit from _____. _____
18. Circumnavigation, _____, is an arduous task. _____
19. His keen sense of smell is useful for _____. _____
20. Today we celebrate _____. _____
21. Kate and Henry decided to postpone _____. _____

© Loyola Press. Voyages in English Grade 7

For additional help, review pages 90–91 in your textbook or visit www.voyagesinenglish.com.

5.5 Possessives with Gerunds, Using -ing Verb Forms

Gerunds may be preceded by a possessive form—either a possessive noun or a possessive adjective. These possessives describe the doer of the action of the gerund.

Circle the word that correctly completes each sentence.

1. (Me   My) agreeing to the decision was a mistake.

2. (Dad   Dad's) cracking his knuckles made me wince.

3. (Dana's   Dana) slamming the door woke everyone up.

4. She did not understand her (friend   friend's) rejecting the ideas for the project.

5. (We   Our) finishing the hallway mural on time was a good idea.

6. (Tim's   Tim) winning the race made him the conference champion.

Write whether the italicized word in each sentence is used as a gerund (*G*), a participial adjective (*A*), or a participle in a verb phrase (*P*).

7. I hope I have the *winning* raffle ticket. _____

8. *Winning* the raffle was a surprise. _____

9. Carla practiced *sprinting* for the big race. _____

10. She was *thanking* her family for their support and encouragement. _____

11. *Sitting* on the edge of our seats, we waited to see what would happen next. _____

12. The clown was *juggling* six basketballs at once. _____

Write a sentence using each word as a gerund, a participle, or a verb in the progressive tense. Then write how you used the word.

13. running: _____

Word used as _____.

14. shining: _____

Word used as _____.

15. making: _____

Word used as _____.

16. finishing: _____

Word used as _____.

For additional help, review pages 92–93 in your textbook or visit www.voyagesinenglish.com.

5.6 Infinitives as Subjects and Subject Complements

An **infinitive** is a verb form, usually preceded by *to*, that is used as a noun, an adjective, or an adverb.

Underline each infinitive or infinitive phrase. Write whether the infinitive is used as a *subject* or a *subject complement*.

1. To complain is a waste of time.   _____

2. Her wish is to travel throughout Europe.   _____

3. To tell the truth was the best choice.   _____

4. His primary goal is to do the best job he can.   _____

5. To express your emotions is healthy.   _____

6. Our first goal is to visit the Grand Canyon.   _____

7. My plan for getting the role is to practice my lines.   _____

8. To swim in a tropical lagoon would be a wonderful thing.   _____

9. To snowboard should be quite exciting.   _____

10. The purpose of the poster is to symbolize freedom.   _____

Write an infinitive or infinitive phrase to complete each sentence. Write if the infinitive is used as a subject (*S*) or a subject complement (*SC*).

11. _____ was common in the Old West.   _____

12. The goal of many people is _____.   _____

13. _____ is a challenge for many students.   _____

14. _____ is often a requirement for success.   _____

15. A precursor for victory in any race is _____. _____

16. _____ was needed for combustion to occur.   _____

17. Another useful character trait is _____.   _____

18. Henderson's primary talent was _____.   _____

19. _____ is key to traveling safely.   _____

20. One way to see the world would be _____.   _____

21. _____ is a task for most motivated students. _____

22. A wish I have had for a long time is _____.   _____

For additional help, review pages 94–95 in your textbook or visit www.voyagesinenglish.com.

5.7 Infinitives as Objects

An infinitive functioning as a noun can be used as a direct object in a sentence. This direct object may be preceded by a noun or pronoun. The infinitive and its subject form an **infinitive clause.**

Underline the infinitive used as a direct object in each sentence.

1. The builders wanted to support the roof by reinforcing the walls.

2. The suspect wrote to confess to the crime.

3. John intended to propose to Mary on the transcontinental train trip.

4. The children were taught to tolerate different points of view.

5. Adelle continued to deny any involvement in the prank.

Underline the infinitive, infinitive phrase, or infinitive clause in each sentence. Circle the verb of which each is the direct object.

6. The old cat loved to abandon its toys in the middle of the carpet.

7. The club president needs to increase recognition for the club in the school.

8. Carrie tried to understand the complex construction of the sentence.

9. Rolph wanted to watch his favorite movie over and over.

10. We regret to inform you that your application to Upstart Academy has been denied.

Underline each infinitive used as a noun. Write whether the infinitive is used as a subject (*S*), a subject complement (*SC*), or a direct object (*DO*).

11. The missionaries wanted to build a school.   _____

12. My plan for vacation is to read several books.   _____

13. To study for two hours each night is my goal for this week.   _____

14. We agreed that the best option was to postpone the trip.   _____

15. The politician promised to make the public aware of the issues.   _____

16. To cross the finish line was my goal.   _____

17. When did you decide to administer the test?   _____

18. The guests expected to return to their seats.   _____

19. The substitute teacher's first task was to take attendance.   _____

20. Roger's first task is to find an answer to all his questions.   _____

On another sheet of paper, write three sentences using infinitives. Use one infinitive as a subject, one as a subject complement, and one as a direct object.

© Loyola Press. Voyages in English   Grade 7

For additional help, review pages 96–97 in your textbook or visit www.voyagesinenglish.com.

5.8 Infinitives as Appositives

An infinitive functioning as a noun can be used as an appositive. An **appositive** is a word or group of words used after a noun or pronoun to rename it and give more information about it.

Underline the infinitive phrase used as an appositive in each sentence. Then circle the word that each appositive explains.

1. It was the actor's role, to make the audience laugh, that he accomplished best.

2. Her endeavor, to climb the world's tallest mountain, will take much preparation.

3. Our dream, to visit all the U.S. national parks, will come true someday.

4. Tia's kindness, to help the small child, earned her respect from her parents.

5. Dillan's assignment, to write a short story, is due in two weeks.

6. The country's need, to conserve natural resources, requires everyone's commitment.

7. Miguel's goal, to win the spelling championship, occupies a great deal of his time.

8. The agreement, to share the money equally, pleased both sides.

9. The children's reward, to visit the amusement park, was well deserved.

10. Our objective, to improve school spirit, proved most difficult.

11. The president's oath, to serve our country, is an essential part of the inauguration.

12. My primary focus, to keep from getting seasick, did not last long.

Underline each infinitive or infinitive phrase. Write whether the infinitive is used as a *subject*, a *subject complement*, a *direct object*, or an *appositive*.

13. To allow sweets was more than the nanny would allow. _____

14. Our hope, to walk the deck before night fell, was thwarted. _____

15. The king was permitted to rule the country. _____

16. To suggest cooperation seemed disloyal. _____

17. Julie tried to prevent the captain's escape. _____

18. The cook's idea, to invite Karen for dinner, was a good one. _____

19. Eva's greatest fault, to argue every point, annoyed us all. _____

20. The purpose of the signs was to warn us of the danger. _____

21. Javier strained to picture the next season. _____

On another sheet of paper, write three sentences that each use an infinitive as a noun.

© Loyola Press. Voyages in English **Grade 7**

For additional help, review pages 98–99 in your textbook or visit www.voyagesinenglish.com.

6.3 Comparative and Superlative Adverbs

Some adverbs can be compared. These adverbs have **comparative** and **superlative** forms.

Underline the adverb that correctly completes each sentence.

1. Josh (thoughtfully   more thoughtfully) brought Helena some ice for her wounded knee.

2. My brother accepted the apology (graciously   more graciously) than I had expected.

3. Our wood stove heats the house (more efficiently   most efficiently) than the electric heater.

4. The director's movie premiered (earliest   earlier) this week at the new theater.

5. Winter seemed to arrive (sooner   soonest) than expected this year.

Complete the chart by writing the missing forms of each adverb.

POSITIVE	COMPARATIVE	SUPERLATIVE
6. _____	_____	latest
7. _____	better	_____
8. happily	_____	_____
9. _____	worse	_____
10. _____	more/less fluently	_____
11. much	_____	_____
12. _____	_____	longest
13. little	_____	_____

Complete each sentence with an adverb from the chart above and the form indicated in parentheses.

14. History is the subject I like _____. (superlative)

15. Dana did _____ on this test than on the last one. (comparative)

16. Margie slept _____ of all the campers. (superlative)

17. He volunteered _____ than Pedro did. (comparative)

18. I _____ accepted the job of stage manager. (positive)

19. The new student reads this difficult text _____ than I can. (comparative)

For additional help, review pages 114–115 in your textbook or visit www.voyagesinenglish.com.

Section 6 • 73

6.4 Troublesome Words

Troublesome adverbs are those adverbs that are commonly confused and often incorrectly used. When you use these adverbs in your writing, slow down and check that you are using the correct adverb.

Underline the correct word in parentheses to complete each sentence.

1. I found my name (further   farther) down the list.

2. (There   They're) ready to ship the packages tomorrow.

3. After so much training, Liz draws really (well   good).

4. Her paintings are (well   good).

5. I feel (bad   badly) about not studying for the spelling test.

6. Will you be going to (there   their) garage sale?

7. Alma gets along (well   good) with her brother.

8. The old carpet was (bad   badly) worn in several spots.

9. The family will go (they're   there) at the end of the vacation.

10. If you want an apple, here is a (well   good) one.

11. Do you have (they're   their) CDs?

12. Both soccer teams played (well   good).

13. We researched the issue (farther   further) before voting on it.

14. Mom was upset that the baby behaved (bad   badly) during the show.

Complete each sentence with _there_, _their_, or _they're_.

15. Max, Malachi, and Jacob are packing _____ things for a camping trip.

16. _____ going to Seven Mountains with the scouts.

17. Max says he loves to go _____ even though there are bears.

18. _____ black bears searching for food.

19. The scouts are very careful not to leave food out _____.

20. Malachi and Jacob are bringing _____ compasses.

21. _____ hoping to earn an orienteering merit badge.

22. _____ enthusiasm is growing for the camping trip.

23. _____ is always an adventure waiting for them at Seven Mountains.

© Loyola Press. Voyages in English   **Grade 7**

For additional help, review pages 116–117 in your textbook or visit www.voyagesinenglish.com.

6.4   Troublesome Words

Troublesome adverbs are those adverbs that are commonly confused and often incorrectly used. When you use these adverbs in your writing, slow down and check that you are using the correct adverb.

Complete each sentence with *farther* or *further*.

1. With the binoculars we could see _____ than before.

2. We had to walk _____ than we wanted.

3. We agreed there was nothing _____ to say on the subject.

4. Is it _____ to the state of Washington or to Washington, D.C., from here?

5. This strange concept could not be _____ from the truth.

Complete each sentence with *good* or *well*.

6. We wanted to see _____ examples of modern art, so we went to the museum.

7. The twins behaved _____ at the dentist, so we all got to go to a movie.

8. Micah executes karate moves _____ because he has a black belt.

9. The entire class had _____ attendance, so we earned extra credit.

10. Eden explained _____ how to multiply fractions.

Complete each sentence with *bad* or *badly*.

11. The music was discordant and _____ played.

12. I felt _____ about losing Sara's car keys.

13. Fuzzy was not a _____ dog; in fact, he was easy to train.

14. The food was _____, but the conversation was excellent.

15. The planning was thorough, but it was _____ executed.

Write a sentence using each word as an adverb.

16. farther _____

17. further _____

18. well _____

19. badly _____

20. there _____

For additional help, review pages 116–117 in your textbook or visit www.voyagesinenglish.com.

6.5 Adverb Phrases and Clauses

Prepositional phrases used as adverbs to describe verbs, adjectives, or other adverbs are called **adverb phrases.** A dependent clause that acts as an adverb is called an **adverb clause.**

Underline each adverb phrase. Circle the word or words the phrase describes.

1. Many different ingredients complement each other in a recipe.

2. Holly contributes many ideas to the class.

3. Iron and carbon are forged together in a steel mill.

4. During the summer I earn money babysitting my younger brothers.

5. Julie uses nutmeg in casseroles, desserts, and even hot cocoa.

Underline each adverb clause. Circle the word or words the clause describes.

6. Until Henry needed to return home, he helped Mrs. McGillicuty.

7. The gyroscope stabilizes when it spins faster.

8. If there is a snowstorm tonight, school will be canceled.

9. While the children sing for the program, the group will perform a simple dance.

10. The spinning tires slip when they pass over the thin layer of ice.

Write an adverb phrase to complete the first sentence in each pair. Then write an adverb clause to complete the second sentence.

11. It snowed _____.

    It snowed _____.

12. The knight fought the dragon _____.

    The knight fought the dragon _____.

13. We slept _____.

    We slept _____.

14. Paulo will paint _____.

    Paulo will paint _____.

15. Jen can skate faster _____.

    Jen can skate faster _____.

16. We left for the airport _____.

    We left for the airport _____.

For additional help, review pages 118–119 in your textbook or visit www.voyagesinenglish.com.

SECTION 7 | Daily Maintenance

7.1 **The smiling graduates marched proudly across the stage.**
1. Which word is a participial adjective? _____
2. Which word is an adverb? _____
3. Is it an adverb of time, manner, or place? _____
4. What is the adverb phrase? _____
5. Diagram the sentence on another sheet of paper.

7.2 **Linda's new job, working with rescue dogs, is very interesting.**
1. What is the gerund phrase? _____
2. How does it function in the sentence? _____
3. Which word is an adverb? _____
4. Is it an adverb of degree, time, or affirmation? _____
5. Diagram the sentence on another sheet of paper.

7.3 **Why did you choose to apply for the coaching position?**
1. What is the infinitive phrase? _____
2. How does it function in the sentence? _____
3. Which word is an interrogative adverb? _____
4. Which word is a participial adjective? _____
5. Diagram the sentence on another sheet of paper.

7.4 **My sister Laura sings more beautifully than I.**
1. What is the adverb? _____
2. Is the adverb comparative or superlative? _____
3. How is the word *Laura* used in the sentence? _____
4. What is the person of the pronoun *I?* _____
5. Diagram the sentence on another sheet of paper.

7.5 **Domingo plays best after he practices with his piano teacher.**
1. Which word is an adverb? _____
2. What word does it describe? _____
3. Is the adverb comparative or superlative? _____
4. Which word is a proper noun? _____
5. Diagram the sentence on another sheet of paper.

7.6 **When I feel sad, I write songs and poems.**
1. What is the adverb clause? _____
2. Which word does it describe? _____
3. Which words are the direct objects? _____
4. Are the verbs regular or irregular? _____
5. Diagram the sentence on another sheet of paper.

© Loyola Press. Voyages in English   **Grade 7**

7.1 Single and Multiword Prepositions

A **preposition** is a word that shows the relationship between a noun or a pronoun and some other word in a sentence.

Underline each prepositional phrase. Circle each preposition.

1. Many species of jellyfish are found throughout the world's oceans.

2. According to one source, jellyfish are also known as medusa.

3. The jellyfish that are common to most coastal waters are the scyphozoan jellyfish.

4. During the spring, the number of jellyfish increases in response to an increase in food.

5. Over the course of the summer, jellyfish remain plentiful.

6. Because of the decline in food sources, jellyfish numbers decline in the fall and winter.

7. Jellyfish function by means of a web of nerves; they have no brain.

8. Instead of lungs, they simply absorb oxygen from the water around them.

9. Jellyfish may move through the water with contractions and stretches, but many simply float with the current.

10. Young jellyfish are tiny polyps that attach to the sea bottom.

11. When they reach a couple of millimeters, they float off into the water.

12. Most jellyfish aren't dangerous, but people avoid them on account of their painful sting.

Complete each sentence with a single or multiword preposition.

13. My mother and I walked _____ the garden, looking for her missing earring.

14. The train sped _____ the tunnel, illuminating the old stone walls.

15. I plan to study French _____ Spanish, as long as they both fit in my schedule.

16. We packed the clothes _____ our new suitcases and hoped for the best.

17. The outdoor concert was canceled _____ the weather.

18. _____ my brother, we are supposed to meet at Joseph's house tonight.

19. _____ the water main break, the entire student body was sent home.

20. I decided to wear my old jeans _____ a pair of shorts.

21. _____ the brilliant sunshine, it was only 15 degrees that day.

On another sheet of paper, write three sentences that each use a preposition. Use at least one multiword preposition.

For additional help, review pages 124–125 in your textbook or visit www.voyagesinenglish.com.

Section 7 • 79

7.2 Troublesome Prepositions

Troublesome prepositions are commonly misused. Carefully consider the meanings of troublesome prepositions to determine which one fits the context of your writing.

Underline the misused preposition in each sentence.

1. Mike did not want Julia to be angry at herself.

2. Beside Mike, Ernesto and I were also trying to cheer her up.

3. "Life is as if a race you can't ever win, but you can't stop running," said Julia.

4. "Forgive me if I differ from you," replied Ernie, "but I think life is full of hope."

5. "Sometimes between all those racers, nice guys finish first," submitted Mike.

6. "Some days are breezy and warm and the sun shines all day," I contributed, "like the day was made just to touch your heart."

7. "Choosing my best day from between those this month is not easy," Ernesto pointed out.

8. Mike sat besides me and said, "Sometimes you study hard for a test and you ace it."

9. Julia smiled like she said, "OK, maybe you have a point. Sometimes the glass is half full."

10. "Even better," I said, pulling a water bottle off my backpack, "sometimes the glass is full."

Circle the word or words in parentheses to complete each sentence.

11. The lions were (beside   besides) the giraffes at the zoo.

12. The editor divided the writing assignments (between   among) the five reporters.

13. I had enough money to buy this bicycle (off of   from) my uncle.

14. His parents (differ on   differ from) their approach to discipline.

15. Brittany was (angry with   angry at) her little brother.

16. Leon has his own business (beside   besides) his full-time job.

17. Choosing (among   between) the two desserts was very difficult.

18. Monique swam (like   as if) her life depended on it.

19. Who (beside   besides) the Hendersons are coming to dinner tomorrow night?

20. I kicked the ball (off of   from) where it rested on the grass.

21. The committee's job was to choose (among   between) the five nominees to pick a winner.

22. Lydia's ideas (differ on   differ from) mine when it comes to picking great movies.

23. I (differ from   differ with) my parents on how I should spend my savings.

© Loyola Press. Voyages in English   **Grade 7**

For additional help, review pages 126–127 in your textbook or visit www.voyagesinenglish.com.

8.1 Kinds of Sentences

A **sentence** is a group of words that expresses a complete thought. A sentence consists of a complete subject and a complete predicate. Sentences can be declarative, interrogative, imperative, and exclamatory.

Underline each complete subject once and each complete predicate twice.

1. Alfred Sisley was a French painter in the Impressionist tradition.

2. His English parents supported him during the years of his youth.

3. After the war his family lost everything.

4. Did you know that Sisley's work did not immediately receive recognition?

5. You should see this artist's beautiful work.

6. Sisley's paintings are especially famous for their accurate portrayal of the French countryside.

7. The images of the intense blue skies help me imagine myself in France.

8. Who would not want to be able to paint like that?

Rewrite each declarative sentence as an imperative sentence, an interrogative sentence, and an exclamatory sentence. Add or delete words as needed.

9. The boys are going to plan a picnic.

    Imperative: _____

    Interrogative: _____

    Exclamatory: _____

10. I want you to think about the opportunities.

    Imperative: _____

    Interrogative: _____

    Exclamatory: _____

11. Our homeroom teacher will assign jobs to everyone.

    Imperative: _____

    Interrogative: _____

    Exclamatory: _____

12. It is important to work together on this project.

    Imperative: _____

    Interrogative: _____

    Exclamatory: _____

For additional help, review pages 140–141 in your textbook
or visit www.voyagesinenglish.com.

8.2   Adjective and Adverb Phrases

A **phrase** is a group of words that is used as a single part of speech. A phrase can be prepositional, participial, or infinitive. A phrase often functions as an adjective or an adverb.

Write *PREP* (prepositional), *PART* (participial), or *INF* (infinitive) to identify the italicized phrase in each sentence. Then write *ADV* (adverb) or *ADJ* (adjective) to identify how the phrase is used.

	TYPE OF PHRASE	USED AS
1. Weston remarked that he had never traveled *on a train*.	_____	_____
2. *Telling a happy story*, the speaker laughed.	_____	_____
3. Holt Skating Rink *in the park* was closed today.	_____	_____
4. Allison's bouquet *of flowers* looked beautiful.	_____	_____
5. People came *to see the movie star*.	_____	_____
6. *Feeling tired*, the small child took a nap.	_____	_____
7. Lee looked *in the attic* to find the old trunk.	_____	_____
8. A good time *to get bread* is in the morning.	_____	_____
9. *Running in circles*, the children sang and laughed.	_____	_____
10. Each show ends *with a fireworks display*.	_____	_____

Underline each adjective phrase once and each adverb phrase twice. Write whether each phrase is prepositional (*PREP*), participial (*PART*), or infinitive (*INF*).

11. "Russian mountains" were frozen water over tall wood structures.	_____
12. The mountains were built during the 17th and 18th centuries.	_____
13. No one knows where the idea to build them originated.	_____
14. Rising as high as 80 feet in the air, the mountains were a formidable sight.	_____
15. People rode down the ice mountains on sleds.	_____
16. The mountains inspired rides in other parts of Europe.	_____
17. Using sleds on wheels, these rides predated the modern roller coaster.	_____
18. Roller coasters are a special kind of rail system.	_____
19. The first roller coaster patent was issued on January 20, 1885.	_____
20. Roller coasters have tracks that rise and fall in elevation.	_____
21. Flipping the rider upside down, some designs have inversions.	_____
22. Most modern roller coasters are found in amusement parks.	_____
23. Designers create roller coasters to thrill excited fans.	_____

For additional help, review pages 142–143 in your textbook or visit www.voyagesinenglish.com.

8.3   Adjective Clauses

A **clause** is a group of words that has a subject and a predicate. An independent clause is one that expresses a complete thought and so can stand on its own. A dependent clause cannot stand on its own.

Underline the adjective clause in each sentence. Circle the noun that each adjective clause describes.

1. This bus, which is at our stop, will be going downtown.
2. This is the movie that I told you about.
3. England is the place where the story begins.
4. My sister, whom I took ice-skating, enjoyed her day.
5. That author, whose books are popular with children, will be at our library.
6. Mr. Vogel, who is my favorite teacher, is going on vacation.
7. Spring is the time when birds build their nests.
8. Dominique is the reason why I joined the photography club.
9. Canada is ruled by a constitutional monarch, who is known as the Queen of Canada.
10. Lincoln School, which usually holds its Sports Day in June, is moving the event to May.
11. Carrots, which are easy to grow yourself, are rich in key vitamins.
12. The most surprising feature of the new car, which runs on electricity, is its low cost.

Underline the adjective clause in each sentence. Circle the relative pronoun or subordinate conjunction in the adjective clause.

13. The praying mantis, which is primarily diurnal, relies heavily on its sense of sight.
14. Insects that the praying mantis eats include some agricultural pests.
15. The praying mantis's head, which can turn almost 300 degrees, is heart-shaped.
16. A praying mantis, which uses its grasping fore legs, grabs and holds its live prey.

Write an adjective clause to complete each sentence.

17. This morning, _____, I barely made it to school on time.
18. First, there was the incident with the peanut butter _____.
19. Then my brother, _____, couldn't find his trumpet.
20. Next, my mother couldn't find her keys _____.
21. My hope _____ was seeming pretty far-fetched.
22. We found the trumpet and keys and ran out to the car _____.

© Loyola Press. Voyages in English   Grade 7

For additional help, review pages 144–145 in your textbook
or visit www.voyagesinenglish.com.

8.4 Restrictive and Nonrestrictive Clauses

Restrictive clauses are essential clauses without which a sentence will not make sense. An adjective clause that is not essential to the meaning of a sentence is a **nonrestrictive clause.**

Write if the italicized adjective clause is restrictive (R) or nonrestrictive (N).

1. Ancient Greek theater, *which was well developed by fifth century B.C.*, was very different from attending a modern play.   _____

2. The three men *who were the actors* played all the roles.   _____

3. The venue, *which was always an outdoor theater*, was a large half-circle.   _____

4. The plays *that were produced* were only performed once.   _____

5. Every play, *which was part of a religious festival*, honored Dionysus.   _____

6. The polis, *who were the citizens of Greece*, paid for the production.   _____

7. The plays, *which were highly structured*, competed with other plays for first, second, or third prize.   _____

Underline each restrictive adjective clause once and each nonrestrictive adjective clause twice. Circle the noun to which each adjective clause refers.

8. Kabuki, which is a highly stylized form of Japanese theater, began in the early 17th century.

9. The Kabuki stage, which has special features and machinery, includes a hanamichi, or projection into the audience.

10. Chunori, which adds dramatic effect, lifts an actor into the air.

11. The wires that lift an actor into the air have been in use since the mid-19th century.

12. Seri are a series of stage traps, which raise and lower sets and actors on the stage.

13. The sets that rotate to make scene changes easier are called mawari-butai.

14. These special stage features, which were developed to make sudden plot revelations or character transformations possible, give Kabuki sophistication.

15. A Kabuki play that retells famous moments in Japanese history might go on for a full day.

16. A full-length play is done in five acts, which are each progressively faster in pace.

17. The final act, which should provide a satisfying resolution, is almost always very short.

18. Kabuki actors wear makeup that tells the audience something about their characters.

19. Kabuki actors who are well known by the audience may be rewarded by having members of the audience call out their names or those of their fathers.

For additional help, review pages 146–147 in your textbook or visit www.voyagesinenglish.com.

8.4 Restrictive and Nonrestrictive Clauses

Restrictive clauses are essential clauses without which a sentence will not make sense. An adjective clause that is not essential to the meaning of a sentence is a **nonrestrictive clause.**

Choose and write an adjective clause to complete each sentence. Add commas as needed. Write if the clause is restrictive (R) or nonrestrictive (NR).

whose dog ran away	which grow in ponds and lakes
whose loom I bought	that I just finished reading
that was auctioned	which is famous for cheese production

1. The ball _____ was signed by Michael Jordan. _____

2. Water lilies _____ live on the surface of water. _____

3. The weaver _____ moved to Minnesota. _____

4. Tyrone is the neighbor _____. _____

5. Wisconsin _____ is the country's largest producer of cranberries. _____

6. The biography _____ is excellent. _____

Write a restrictive or nonrestrictive adjective clause to complete each sentence. Add commas where necessary.

7. The pond _____ was stocked with fish.

8. My best friend _____ helped me.

9. Before tomorrow's concert _____ we will be ready.

10. The next game _____ is Friday.

11. The lens _____ captures special memories.

12. The rain _____ canceled our plans.

13. We saw the rainbow _____.

14. Our goal _____ was a worthy one.

15. We cleaned the table _____.

16. The new puppy _____ made us laugh.

For additional help, review pages 146–147 in your textbook or visit www.voyagesinenglish.com.

8.5   Adverb Clauses

An **adverb clause** is a dependent clause used as an adverb. An adverb clause describes or gives information about a verb, an adjective, or an adverb.

Underline the adverb clause in each sentence. Circle the subordinate conjunction.

1. When it is summer in the Northern Hemisphere, it is winter in the Southern Hemisphere.
2. After the time ran out on the clock, the students cheered wildly.
3. Eric will peel the potatoes while we make the salad.
4. Gina wrapped all the presents before she went to bed.
5. Jack cupped his hands around his ears because he couldn't hear the speech.
6. Don't start the test until I give the signal.
7. We smelled the peach cobbler as soon as we entered the restaurant.
8. When I heard the phone ring, I ran into the kitchen to answer it.
9. Although the children were tired, they didn't want to go to bed.

Underline the adverb clause in each sentence. Circle the word or words each adverb clause modifies.

10. As long as the dogs are trained, they can participate in agility competitions.
11. If you and I help, others will volunteer their time too.
12. Since the Parkers like board games so much, they made every Monday game night.
13. During the holiday celebrations, few people worked unless the job was really necessary.
14. When the beverages arrived, we added them to the buffet table.
15. After I clean my room, I plan to play soccer with my friends.
16. The class sang silly songs on the bus wherever we went on the field trip.
17. John wasn't interested in math until he was invited to compete in the contest.

Write an adverb clause to complete each sentence.

18. _____, I plan to attend the party.
19. _____, she usually swims well.
20. The batter has hit the ball harder _____.
21. I often write best _____.
22. _____, Jake will not be able to join you.

© Loyola Press. Voyages in English   **Grade 7**

For additional help, review pages 148–149 in your textbook or visit www.voyagesinenglish.com.

8.6   Noun Clauses as Subjects

Dependent clauses can be used as nouns. These clauses, called **noun clauses,**
typically begin with introductory words such as *how, that, what, whatever, when,
where, whether, who, whoever, whom, whomever,* and *why.*

Underline the noun clause used as a subject in each sentence.

1. That my brother can climb the fence amazes me.

2. Whatever ate the apple is still in the yard.

3. Whoever arrived last left the door wide open.

4. Whomever we pick should already be a member of the club.

5. Why we keep losing the key to the back door is a mystery to me.

6. How this puzzle goes together is bewildering us.

7. What the principal had in mind was a celebration in the multipurpose room.

8. Whoever saw our dog in the field said he still was wearing his collar.

9. What Mr. Alexander did was teach us all a new way to do long division.

10. When we plan to go to the store determines whether there is time for one more game.

11. Whether Joe had wanted to quit the team was forgotten after his winning season.

12. Where the dog escaped in the yard was a puzzle until we found the hole in the fence.

**Choose an introductory word to complete each noun clause. Then underline
the entire noun clause that is used as a subject.**

13. _____ they are going is unknown.

14. _____ the girls did with the treasure is a secret.

15. _____ you want for dessert is fine with me.

16. _____ Joe should feel this way came as a surprise to all of us.

17. _____ no one remembered the homework assignment was hard to explain.

18. _____ the magician made the tiger disappear was all we talked about.

19. _____ has worked at the pool will come back again.

20. _____ they want to visit their parents will be decided later.

21. _____ we ask should already have experience with a hockey stick.

22. _____ owns this book is unclear, but there are ways to find out.

23. _____ he will be arriving is written on the itinerary.

For additional help, review pages 150–151 in your textbook
or visit www.voyagesinenglish.com.

8.7 Noun Clauses as Subject Complements

Like nouns, noun clauses can be used as subject complements.

Underline the noun clause used as a subject complement in each sentence. Circle the subject that the noun clause describes or renames.

1. Michael's greatest achievement was that he earned a scholarship at the technology fair.

2. The question is whether or not Mrs. Holcolmb can drive us all to the game tomorrow.

3. One theory explaining the disappearance of the cake is that the dog ate it.

4. Another suggestion has been that we all go together in one van to save on gas.

5. Something to think about is how we are going to get everyone to the competition.

6. A reason for concern is whether or not it might snow tonight.

Underline the noun clause in each sentence. Indicate if the noun clause is used as a subject (*S*) or as a subject complement (*SC*).

7. What I had for breakfast made me feel better.   _____

8. Her wish was that all her friends could come to the party.   _____

9. The truth was that Mary was faster than Ted.   _____

10. Whatever the teacher said was inspiring.   _____

11. Our main concern at the moment was how to get home before dark. _____

12. The problem was that I forgot my homework.   _____

13. Jay's goal is that he can buy a new amplifier.   _____

14. What role he played is still a puzzle to the committee.   _____

15. That he would win the contest was taken for granted.   _____

16. The second house from the corner is where the Jacobs live. _____

17. One of the school's mysteries is what is behind the locked red door. _____

18. The fact is that February is a good month for ice-skating. _____

Write a noun clause used as a subject complement to complete each sentence.

19. Randall's best character trait was _____.

20. Mrs. Smith's favorite lesson is _____.

21. The best prize is _____.

22. My hope for the future is _____.

© Loyola Press. Voyages in English **Grade 7**

For additional help, review pages 152–153 in your textbook or visit www.voyagesinenglish.com.

9.3 Conjunctive Adverbs

Conjunctive adverbs connect independent clauses. A semicolon is used before the conjunctive adverb, and a comma is used after it. **Parenthetical expressions** are used in the same way as conjunctive adverbs.

Circle the correct conjunctive adverb or parenthetical expression to complete each sentence.

1. My brother plays golf at least once a week; (moreover   however), he often attends golfing classes on the weekend.

2. It was extremely foggy the day of the tour; (later   consequently), we were able to spot very few eagles.

3. I live in an area where groundhogs are common; (furthermore   nevertheless), the first time I saw one I thought it was a beaver.

4. There are many lakes in Minnesota; (in fact   nevertheless), the state's slogan is "Land of 10,000 Lakes."

5. Juanita isn't afraid of roller coasters; (otherwise   on the contrary), she was one of the first people to ride on the Cobra.

6. We have spent a long time on our homework; (finally   still), we can't solve the last two problems.

7. Gwen has always liked math and is very good at it; (however   therefore), she plans to become a math teacher.

8. Nate enjoys playing soccer and tennis; (besides   however), he has decided to try out for only one team.

9. Bob's Smoke Pit has great food; (indeed   therefore), it has the best ribs in town.

10. Our cabin is in the mountains; (however   therefore), we see many wild animals.

11. Danielle doesn't want to make a ceramic pot; (moreover   instead), she plans to make a large serving platter.

12. The waves are too high for surfing; (besides   consequently), the water is too cold.

Write a conjunctive adverb to complete each sentence.

13. Inventors are interested in things that make our lives easier; _____, many inventions are intended for use in the home.

14. Most dogs were working animals; _____, they were bred for specific jobs.

15. On the conductor's command, an orchestra may begin playing; _____, the musicians follow the conductor's signals for pace and volume.

16. Abby is getting good grades; _____, she wants to do even better.

For additional help, review pages 170–171 in your textbook or visit www.voyagesinenglish.com.

Section 9 • 105

9.4 Subordinate Conjunctions

A **subordinate conjunction** is used to join an independent clause and a dependent clause.

Underline the subordinate conjunction in each sentence.

1. Because the understudy knew her lines, the show was saved.
2. We brought two balls so that we would have a spare ready.
3. If anyone hosted a party, the neighbors were sure to show up.
4. Elliot's talent was in baseball, while Adam's talent was in football.
5. John jumped around the room, waving his arms as if he were playing a guitar.

Circle the subordinate conjunction in each sentence. Underline the dependent clause.

6. She acts as if nothing is wrong.
7. While they were in New York, it snowed 20 inches.
8. The basketball team forfeited the game because not enough players showed up.
9. We used bright colors so that our signs would stand out from the others.
10. Ellen has been driving to school since she turned 18.
11. I prefer tomatoes when they have ripened on the vine.
12. Trina skated better than she had ever skated before.
13. Why don't we wait here until it is time to leave?
14. After Chris heard about the accident, he rushed to the hospital.
15. When we visited Yosemite, we hiked to the top of Half Dome.
16. Although I like this dress, I cannot afford to buy it.
17. Kim will go to the concert even though she has not finished her homework.

Complete each sentence with an appropriate dependent clause beginning with a subordinate conjunction.

18. _____, they were ready to go to the movies.
19. _____, many people see a dentist twice a year.
20. _____, Julie did her homework every night.
21. _____, Ty grew to enjoy the talks with his aunt.
22. _____, you might be late for sports practice.
23. _____, the group decided to continue sledding.

© Loyola Press. Voyages in English   Grade 7

For additional help, review pages 172–173 in your textbook or visit www.voyagesinenglish.com.

9.5 Troublesome Conjunctions

Some conjunctions are frequently misused or confused.

Write *without* or *unless* to complete each sentence.

1. _____ proper storage, the lawn mower may rust over the winter.

2. Don't pick up that book _____ you have the time to read the entire thing.

3. _____ we find a used part for the car, we won't be able to leave on our trip.

4. The animal will not thrive _____ sufficient food and water.

5. Buy three tickets for the show _____ your sister says she doesn't want to go.

6. _____ my brothers in the house, it is very quiet around here.

7. _____ more parents can attend, the field trip will have to be canceled.

Circle the correct item to complete each sentence.

8. (Unless   Without) his bus pass, he will not be able to ride the bus today.

9. I read through the magazine (as   like) I waited.

10. He acted (like   as if) he didn't get enough sleep.

11. Don't leave (unless   without) I call you first.

12. The huge snake looked (like   as if) a tree branch in the sand.

13. A computer won't work (unless   without) you plug it in.

14. (Unless   Without) the weather gets colder, we won't be able to go ice-skating.

15. I felt (like   as if) nothing could go wrong.

16. The climbers grew weary (like   as) the guide led them along the steep paths.

17. Our car looked (like   as if) no one had washed it in quite some time.

18. Gary ordered a sandwich (unless   without) onions or pickles.

19. The sound of the katydids in the trees was (like   as if) that of rain on the canopy.

Rewrite each sentence to correct the use of conjunctions and prepositions.

20. The dogs were barking like there was a stranger in the yard.

_____

21. The birds made their nest in the old wasps' nest, like my friend told me.

_____

22. You must see the high school building, which looks as a huge cement block.

_____

© Loyola Press. Voyages in English   Grade 7

For additional help, review pages 174–175 in your textbook or visit www.voyagesinenglish.com.

9.6   Interjections

An **interjection** is a word that expresses a strong or sudden emotion.

Circle the interjection that is the best match for each sentence.

1. (Yikes   Yum), that had to hurt!

2. (Wow   No)! That last fireworks display was the best.

3. (Hello   Enough)! It's time to end the game and go inside.

4. (Sh   Oh, no)! The baby is finally asleep.

5. (Bravo   Hush)! That was an excellent story for such a young author.

6. (Beware   Good grief), I really thought that she was going to steal second base!

7. (Gosh   Hooray)! I thought I had more money than this.

8. (Ha   Indeed)! That trick worked really well this time.

9. (Hush   Whew)! The bell will ring in just one more minute.

Write a sentence with an interjection to match each situation.

10. a server in a restaurant who just dropped a tray of food

_____

11. a construction worker who hit his thumb with a hammer

_____

12. a librarian quieting children

_____

13. a scientist making an important discovery

_____

14. a child tasting her favorite food

_____

15. a person watching trapeze artists at a circus

_____

16. a student who discovers that she has forgotten her homework

_____

17. a customer politely seeking the attention of a salesclerk

_____

For additional help, review pages 176–177 in your textbook or visit www.voyagesinenglish.com.

SECTION 10 Daily Maintenance

10.1 **A goldfish or a gerbil is a good pet for most children.**
1. Is the sentence or the subject compound? _____
2. What is the correlative conjunction? _____
3. Which word is a subject complement? _____
4. What is the adjective phrase? _____
5. Diagram the sentence on another sheet of paper.

10.2 **Silvia studied for the English test; however, she made several errors.**
1. Is the sentence simple, compound, or complex? _____
2. What is the conjunctive adverb? _____
3. What is the adverb phrase? _____
4. Which word is an indefinite adjective? _____
5. Diagram the sentence on another sheet of paper.

10.3 **When I lived in Canada, I often visited Lake Louise.**
1. Is the sentence simple, compound, or complex? _____
2. What is the subordinate conjunction? _____
3. What is the adverb clause? _____
4. Which word is an adverb? _____
5. Diagram the sentence on another sheet of paper.

10.4 **Liam cannot go unless his parents give their permission.**

1. Is the sentence simple, compound, or complex? _____
2. What is the subordinate conjunction? _____
3. What is the independent clause? _____
4. Which words are possessive adjectives? _____
5. Diagram the sentence on another sheet of paper.

10.5 **Wow! Lin's illustrations for this book look exquisite.**

1. What is the adjective phrase in the sentence? _____
2. What is the linking verb? _____
3. What is the subject complement? _____
4. What is the interjection? _____
5. Diagram the sentence on another sheet of paper.

10.1 Periods and Commas

A **period** is used at the end of a declarative or an imperative sentence, after an abbreviation, and after the initials in a name. **Commas** are used in a variety of ways to separate or set off words, phrases, and clauses.

Add commas where needed in these sentences. Then write the letter of the comma rule used in each sentence.

A. to separate words in a series

B. to set off nonrestrictive phrases and clauses

C. to set off words of direct address

D. to set off parenthetical expressions

E. to set off dates

F. to set off place names

G. to set off divided quotations

1. "After you finish your homework" said Maria "I have a surprise for you."   _____

2. He was born in Fairbanks Alaska but he now lives in Seattle Washington.   _____

3. The package will be there I promise you by next Tuesday.   _____

4. Myra I can't make it to the play tonight.   _____

5. The Declaration of Independence was signed on July 4 1776.   _____

6. Ronald Reagan who had once been an actor became our 40th president.   _____

7. Theresa went to the grocery store and bought bread milk and cheese.   _____

Rewrite the sentences to correct any errors in punctuation.

8. I e-mailed Ms Emily Rayward, with my decision on Sept, 15.

_____

9. A local lawyer Mr Richard Kanton was quoted in the newspaper article yesterday

_____

10. Emma made an appointment with Dr Richardson for May 4. 2017

_____

11. Tussey Mountain near State College Penn is home to a small ski resort

_____

12. Yes Lilly, we do need to stop in Athens Georgia on the way home.

_____

© Loyola Press. Voyages in English **Grade 7**

For additional help, review pages 182–183 in your textbook or visit www.voyagesinenglish.com.

10.2 Exclamation Points, Question Marks, Semicolons, and Colons

Exclamation points are used after interjections and exclamatory sentences. **Question marks** are used to end interrogative sentences. **Semicolons** and **colons** are used in specific situations.

Add semicolons and colons where needed.

1. The singer used a microphone nevertheless, we couldn't hear him.
2. Dear Dr. Greenbaum
3. Sheila rides her bike to school I prefer to walk.
4. There was a blizzard last night hence, school was closed.
5. To Whom It May Concern
6. Please call these people Marvin, Jane, Anita, and Martha.
7. Joyce has three favorite hobbies namely, they are knitting, dancing, and rock climbing.
8. I will visit three countries this summer Greece, Spain, and Italy.

Add periods, question marks, or exclamation points where needed.

9. Hey, I can't believe you did that
10. Oh, no What kind of weather can we expect tomorrow
11. What is that strange lump I see in the snow
12. What interesting sights we can see through the Hubble Telescope
13. I decided to call everyone in my class for a party next Friday
14. Ah-ha I believe we have found the culprit who raided the cookie jar
15. Yikes Is that how far we have to run for the physical fitness test

Write a sentence for each topic. Use the correct punctuation.

16. a question about a vacation you would like to take

_____

17. an exclamation that shows happiness

_____

18. a question about your favorite subject

_____

19. an exclamation that is a warning

_____

© Loyola Press. Voyages in English **Grade 7**

For additional help, review pages 184–185 in your textbook or visit www.voyagesinenglish.com.

10.3 Quotation Marks and Italics

Quotation marks are used with direct quotations and for titles of shorter works, such as short stories, poems, and songs. **Italics** are used for titles of books, magazines, newspapers, movies, TV series, and works of art and for the names of ships and aircraft.

Add quotation marks and other punctuation where needed. Use underlining to indicate italics.

1. Where can I park my bicycle asked Isaac.

2. Sylvia selected the short story called The Lottery.

3. I am reading an article titled Budgeting for Teens in Family and Home Magazine.

4. No I'm sorry replied the clerk, but Watership Down is not currently in stock.

5. The boys left here just a half hour ago, said Mrs. Crosby.

6. Wow Look how high his paper airplane flew yelled Marcus.

7. I cannot find the book A Tree Grows in Brooklyn anywhere.

8. Becky suggested, We could all go to my house to practice for the play

Write a sentence for each topic. Include a title in your sentence. Underline words to indicate italics where needed.

9. your favorite movie

_____

10. your favorite television show

_____

11. your favorite book

_____

12. your favorite magazine

_____

13. a song that you like

_____

14. a poem you have read

_____

15. a magazine article you would like to write

_____

© Loyola Press. Voyages in English   Grade 7

For additional help, review pages 186–187 in your textbook or visit www.voyagesinenglish.com.

Section 10 • 113

10.4 Apostrophes, Hyphens, and Dashes

Apostrophes, hyphens, and **dashes** are used to clarify text for the reader.

Circle the letter that correctly explains the punctuation mark that is needed in each sentence. Then add the punctuation mark to the sentence.

1. I turned my head it was only for a second and missed the final shot of the game.
   a. A hyphen is used to separate parts of some compound words.
   b. A dash is used to set off words that indicate a change in thought.

2. The mansion has twenty two rooms.
   a. A hyphen is used in compound numbers between twenty-one and ninety-nine.
   b. A dash is used to set off an appositive.

3. Sandy regularly borrows items from her sisters wardrobe.
   a. An apostrophe shows possession.
   b. An apostrophe is used to show the plurals of lowercase but not of capital letters, unless the plural could be mistaken for a word.

4. Call Raquel she's on the prom committee to get the directions.
   a. A dash is used to set off an appositive that contains commas.
   b. A dash is used to set off words that indicate a change in thought.

5. The *ts* were crossed, and the *is* were dotted.
   a. An apostrophe is used to show the plurals of lowercase but not of capital letters, unless the plural could be mistaken for a word.
   b. An apostrophe shows possession.

Write a sentence for each description, using correct punctuation.

6. An apostrophe shows possession.

   _____

7. A dash is used to set off words that indicate a change in thought.

   _____

8. A hyphen is used in compound numbers between twenty-one and ninety-nine.

   _____

9. A hyphen is used to form some temporary adjectives.

   _____

For additional help, review pages 188–189 in your textbook or visit www.voyagesinenglish.com.

10.5 Capitalization

Using **capital letters** correctly provides valuable clues for the reader that make your writing easier to understand.

Use the proofreading symbol (≡) to show which letters should be capitalized.

1. my mother likes to watch old westerns.

2. usually, i won't watch them with her because i prefer more modern movies.

3. last week a huge snowstorm hit my town, plainview, minnesota.

4. alice, xander, and i went sledding, and my dad took me out on his snowmobile.

5. plainview isn't a very big town though, and everything was closed.

6. finally, i said, "i've been thinking, mom, that we should watch one of your movies."

7. she introduced me to john wayne and jack ely.

8. the towns all had names like dry gulch, deadwood, and windmill junction.

9. all in all, it wasn't a bad way to spend a day with my mother.

Write a sentence that illustrates each rule for using a capital letter.

10. a title when it precedes a person's name

_____

11. the first word in a sentence

_____

12. a direction when it refers to a part of the country

_____

13. an abbreviation of a word that is capitalized

_____

14. a proper noun

_____

15. a proper adjective

_____

16. the principal words in the title of a book, play, or poem

_____

17. the first word of a direct quotation

_____

© Loyola Press. Voyages in English Grade 7

For additional help, review pages 190–191 in your textbook or visit www.voyagesinenglish.com.

SECTION 11 | Daily Maintenance

11.1 **Brandy served her father the largest piece of steak.**
1. How is the word *father* used in the sentence? _____
2. Is the verb regular or irregular? _____
3. What kind of adjective is the word *largest?* _____
4. How is the word *piece* used in the sentence? _____
5. Diagram the sentence on another sheet of paper.

11.2 **Stephen King, an author of many novels, is my favorite writer.**
1. What does the appositive rename? _____
2. Is the appositive restrictive or nonrestrictive? _____
3. Which noun is the object of a preposition? _____
4. How is the word *writer* used in the sentence? _____
5. Diagram the sentence on another sheet of paper.

11.3 **The students have studied weather, and now they will make a rain gauge.**
1. Is the sentence simple, compound, or complex? _____
2. Which word is a coordinating conjunction? _____
3. Which words are direct objects? _____
4. Which word is an adverb? _____
5. Diagram the sentence on another sheet of paper.

11.4 **The small birds collect blades of grass and weave them into nests.**
1. What is the complete subject? _____
2. Is the subject or the predicate compound? _____
3. What is the antecedent of the word *them?* _____
4. Which words are prepositions? _____
5. Diagram the sentence on another sheet of paper.

11.3 Compound Sentences

A **compound sentence** contains two or more independent clauses. An independent clause has a subject and a predicate and can stand on its own as a sentence.

Diagram the sentences.

1. The tourists visited Washington, D.C., and they toured the Lincoln Memorial.

2. Megan ordered a new computer, but it was delivered to her previous address.

3. Emanuel's stories are creative; however, they are often based on real events.

4. Maria prefers autobiographies, yet she frequently reads adventure stories.

© Loyola Press. Voyages in English   Grade 7

For additional help, review pages 200–201 in your textbook or visit www.voyagesinenglish.com.

11.4 Compound Sentence Elements

The subject and the predicate in a sentence may be compound. They may consist of two or more words connected by a coordinating conjunction.

Diagram the sentences.

1. This old silk pillow is smooth and soft.

2. Molly and Grace make their own beds and fold their own laundry.

3. The club president called or visited each member of the committee.

4. Craig and Joe wrote the music and the lyrics for this song.

For additional help, review pages 202–203 in your textbook or visit www.voyagesinenglish.com.

11.5 Participles

A **participle** is a verb form that is used as an adjective. A participial phrase is made up of the participle, its objects or complements, and any modifiers. The entire phrase acts as an adjective.

Diagram the sentences.

1. A smiling woman opened the locked door.

2. Tripping over the exposed tree root, I fell backwards.

3. The Renoir painting, displayed in a room with an expensive security system, is priceless.

4. Walking through the garden, we saw blooming flowers in a wide range of colors.

© Loyola Press. Voyages in English   Grade 7

For additional help, review pages 204–205 in your textbook or visit www.voyagesinenglish.com.

11.6 Gerunds

A **gerund** is a verb form ending in -*ing* that is used as a noun. A gerund can be used in a sentence as a subject, a subject complement, an object of a verb, an object of a preposition, or an appositive.

Diagram the sentences.

1. Diagramming sentences is a useful writing tool.

2. Gabe and T.J. enjoyed playing the game.

3. Miles easily won the competition by creating the best robot.

4. My goal, earning money for college, will require hard work.

For additional help, review pages 206–207 in your textbook or visit www.voyagesinenglish.com.

© Loyola Press. Voyages in English   **Grade 7**

11.7 Infinitives

An **infinitive** is a verb form, usually preceded by *to*, that is used as a noun, an adjective, or an adverb.

Diagram the sentences.

1. Our soccer team wants to score many points in this game.

2. Most students were anxious to see the final test results.

3. My idea, to hold a raffle, will raise money for charity.

4. To survive this powerful storm was their primary concern.

For additional help, review pages 208–209 in your textbook or visit www.voyagesinenglish.com.

11.8 Adjective Clauses

An **adjective clause** is a dependent clause that describes a noun or a pronoun. An adjective clause begins with a relative pronoun or with a subordinate conjunction.

Diagram the sentences.

1. Jim gave her the ring that he had brought from London.

2. This is the woman whose dog won the blue ribbon.

3. The artist who painted this lovely portrait lives in Mexico.

4. The department store where my brother currently works is having a sale.

© Loyola Press. Voyages in English   Grade 7

For additional help, review pages 210–211 in your textbook or visit www.voyagesinenglish.com.

11.9 | Adverb Clauses

An **adverb clause** is a dependent clause that acts as an adverb; it describes a verb, an adjective, or another adverb. Adverb clauses begin with subordinate conjunctions.

Diagram the sentences.

1. Mrs. Hamaguchi canceled the birthday party because her daughter was sick.

2. Since Toby received the highest test score, he has new confidence in his math skills.

3. If Greg studies for another hour, he will finally finish his homework.

4. Maya's sister will call you whenever she needs a ride to school.

For additional help, review pages 212–213 in your textbook or visit www.voyagesinenglish.com.

11.10 Noun Clauses

Dependent clauses can be used as nouns. **Noun clauses** work in sentences in the same way that nouns do.

Diagram the sentences.

1. Billy now recalls why he kept his notebook from the previous school year.

2. That the animal is dangerous and unpredictable seems obvious.

3. The fact that she was intelligent could not be denied.

4. Whoever uses the new sports equipment should be appreciative.

© Loyola Press. Voyages in English **Grade 7**

For additional help, review pages 214–215 in your textbook or visit www.voyagesinenglish.com.

11.11 Diagramming Practice

Diagramming shows the relationships among words in a sentence. It shows how a sentence is put together.

Read the diagrams and write out the sentences.

1. _____

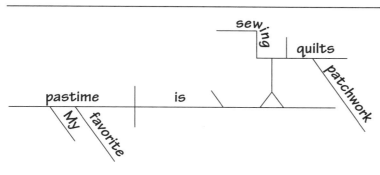

2. _____

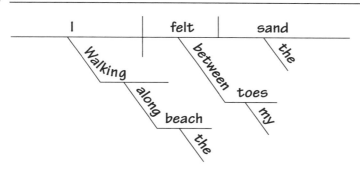

3. _____

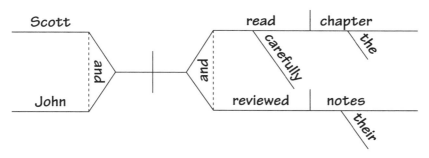

4. _____

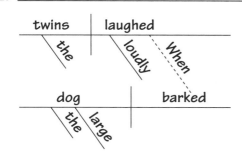

© Loyola Press. Voyages in English   Grade 7

For additional help, review pages 216–217 in your textbook or visit www.voyagesinenglish.com.

What Makes a Good Personal Narrative?

A **personal narrative** is a true story about a particular event written by the person who experienced it.

Read each statement. Circle *T* if the statement is true or *F* if the statement is false. Then rewrite each false statement to make it true.

1. A personal narrative tells about events that really happened.   T   F

   _____

2. A personal narrative is written in the third person.   T   F

   _____

3. The events of a personal narrative are written in a random order.   T   F

   _____

4. A personal narrative should flow smoothly from beginning to end.   T   F

   _____

5. A good topic would be one that the writer thinks is a bit interesting.   T   F

   _____

Write *yes* or *no* to show whether each idea would be an appropriate topic for a personal narrative.

6. instructions on how to build a bookshelf from wood   _____

7. the morning I discovered that someone had stolen my bike   _____

8. my day volunteering at the hospital   _____

9. a tourist's favorite places to visit in Washington, D.C.   _____

Write the tone of each passage.

10. "Stop!" I screamed, as I lunged to grab his jacket.   _____

11. "Look! Spring must be coming. The robin has returned!"   _____

12. Swimming in the warm river, I felt my cares float away.   _____

13. It was a clean snap! The quarterback made a break for it.   _____

14. Suddenly a wave of sorrow seemed to wash over me.   _____

15. I paused at that alley entrance, unable to see a thing.   _____

For additional help, review pages 224–227 in your textbook or visit www.voyagesinenglish.com.

Introduction, Body, and Conclusion

A good personal narrative has an **introduction**, a **body**, and a **conclusion**.

For each part of a personal narrative, write the letter of the matching description.

1. introduction _____   **a.** leaves the reader feeling satisfied and prompts the reader to think

2. body _____   **b.** tells what happened in chronological order

3. conclusion _____   **c.** sets the scene for the narrative

Read these mixed-up sentences from a personal narrative. Number the events in the logical order. Then circle the introduction and underline the conclusion.

4. After I put on my boots and skis, I took a lesson. _____

5. I started down the mountain balancing on one leg. _____

6. I will never forget the first time I went skiing. _____

7. After a two-hour lesson, I felt confident enough to approach the chairlift. _____

8. As I attempted to get out of the chairlift, my left ski came off. _____

9. After that experience, I can safely say that two skis are better than one! _____

10. Luckily, my instructor retrieved my left ski and handed it to me on her way down. _____

11. The ride up on the chairlift made me feel calm as I gazed at the mountain scenery. _____

12. I reached for my left ski, but unfortunately my right ski did not want to stop. _____

13. The mountain scenery remained, but that calm feeling suddenly changed. _____

Write a new introductory sentence for the above personal narrative. Then compare your introduction to the original, and tell how each is alike and different.

_____

_____

Rewrite each sentence to make it a better concluding sentence.

14. I was pretty happy with the way the day turned out.

_____

15. I decided not to go back the next day.

_____

© Loyola Press. Voyages in English   Grade 7

For additional help, review pages 228–231 in your textbook
or visit www.voyagesinenglish.com.

Chapter 1 • 131

Revising Sentences

Revising sentences can help eliminate sentences that ramble or run on. **Rambling sentences** and **run-on sentences** make your writing harder to understand. You can avoid these kinds of sentences by being concise.

Each sentence pair has a rambling sentence and a run-on sentence. Circle the letter of the rambling sentence. Use proofreading marks to correct each sentence.

1. **a.** Larry walked onto the stage his heart began to pound very fast.
   b. He could not speak and he had a look of fear on his face, so Mrs. Burke began whispering his lines to him.

2. **a.** Fifteen students bought sweatshirts with the school logo, but the Pep Club still had dozens left to sell, and they had to be sold by the end of the day.
   b. Shaina had the idea that improved sales each fan received a magnet for every sweatshirt sold.

3. **a.** With the team down by one point and two seconds to go, Jenna was fouled as she went up for the shot, and the ball went in and out of the basket.
   b. The referee handed her the ball at the free-throw line she bounced it four times and then made her first free throw.

4. **a.** One of the first things the new teacher did was smile at each student she wanted each child to feel comfortable.
   b. Little Jamie waited until the bell rang and ran up and gave Miss Cross a picture that he had drawn in class, and Miss Cross taped the picture to her desk.

5. **a.** The women spent the day shopping at the mall and they spotted many bargains, but they did not buy anything.
   b. Ursula looked at the glossy, polished diamond ring in the window the sign noted that the ring was on sale.

Cross out the redundant words in each sentence.

6. She was intent on eliminating and purging the redundant words in her writing.

7. Abby stared into the empty, vacant den and wondered where the wild wolves had gone.

8. Their host was courteous and interesting, while also being polite and sympathetic.

9. The costume was outlandish and bizarre, but Josh wasn't sure what was wrong with that.

10. "Ordinarily," I stammered, "usually we start with a math warm-up and begin the lesson."

11. I was startled and frightened to see that my path was blocked by an enormous, tall man.

© Loyola Press. Voyages in English **Grade 7**

For additional help, review pages 232–235 in your textbook or visit www.voyagesinenglish.com.

LESSON
4

Exact Words

Exact words convey a specific, intended meaning to the reader. Precise words also help create more vivid visual images for the reader.

Circle the two words that are more specific examples of each word in bold type.

1. **house**	home	mansion	shack	residence
2. **animal**	camel	hyena	creature	beast
3. **vehicle**	motorcycle	ride	chariot	transportation
4. **flower**	plant	rose	daisy	blossom
5. **build**	make	form	assemble	construct
6. **strong**	potent	able	robust	big
7. **old**	dated	aged	decrepit	antique
8. **throw**	send	propel	fling	lift
9. **little**	diminutive	small	mini	microscopic
10. **chair**	seat	throne	furniture	recliner

Underline the homophone that correctly completes each sentence.

11. Kate couldn't believe how (callous   callus) the instructor was being.

12. When Raul went to the (sight   cite   site) on the Internet, it crashed his computer.

13. The old house had a laundry (chute   shoot) down which the boys tossed their dirty clothes.

14. I tried to (ring   wring) out the mop into the bucket, but the water went everywhere.

15. The construction workers decided to (raise   raze   rays) the dilapidated building.

Write the homophone that matches each definition. Use a dictionary if necessary.

16. to cover completely; not *rap* but . . .   _____

17. one's appearance; not *presents* but . . .   _____

18. related to the military; not *marshal* but . . .   _____

19. to sell something; not *pedal* but . . .   _____

20. to look back; not *revue* but . . .   _____

21. a juvenile; not *miner* but . . .   _____

22. to be pulled tight; not *taught* but . . .   _____

23. an officer in the army or air force; not *kernel* but . . .   _____

For additional help, review pages 236–239 in your textbook or visit www.voyagesinenglish.com.

Graphic Organizers

A **graphic organizer** can help writers map out their ideas. A graphic organizer can help arrange subtopics and details related to a chosen topic. It also keeps writers from introducing unnecessary details.

Complete the time line. Add only the dates and events you consider most important to your life.

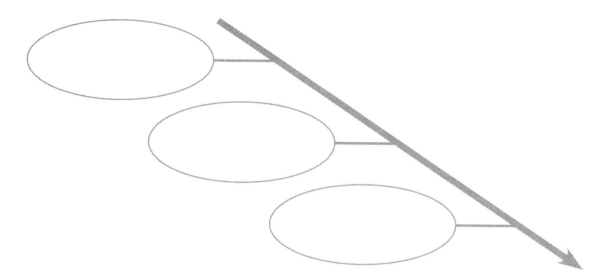

Fill in the word web below using an experience from your own life. Add more ovals if you need to.

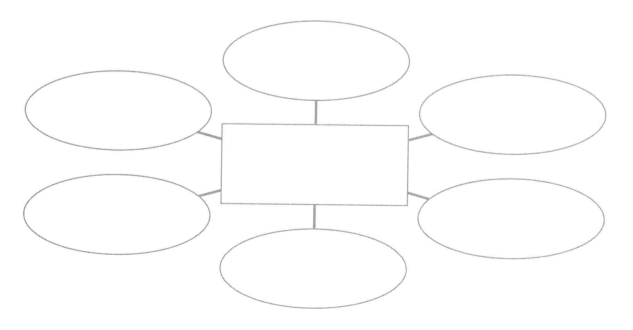

For additional help, review pages 240–243 in your textbook or visit www.voyagesinenglish.com.

What Makes a Good Business Letter?

A **business letter** is a formal letter with a business-related purpose. It includes a heading, an inside address, a salutation, the body, and a closing.

Circle the words that correctly complete the sentences in this paragraph.

A letter of application is a type of (personal   business) letter. It is (a formal   an informal) letter that has a (general   specific) purpose. The purpose of a letter of application is to apply for a (job   license). This kind of letter should always be (long and rambling   short and to the point).

Evaluate the sentences for appropriateness in a business letter. Cross out extraneous information. Then on another sheet of paper, rewrite the sentences that require a more professional tone.

1. I am sooo glad I picked your company from which to buy this little widget!

2. I am writing to express my displeasure with the service I received at store #103 on Tuesday, May 3. Of course, I write a lot of letters, but maybe you will actually answer this one.

3. Hi, I hope this letter finds you well. I am writing to thank you for your company's generous donation to our school fund-raiser. The family fun passes were very popular with bidders.

4. I received my order in the mail today. What were you thinking? This isn't a water dish; it's a swimming pool! I am returning the "dish." Please send me my refund.

5. We admire your company's dedication to the community and want to know how we can help. I really love to sing. Is there any way I can do something like that to help?

6. I am writing to explain my part in the events of last weekend. It is totally unfair that I am being blamed for the damage that was done. It's true I was there, but I was one of the people telling others that they should go find something else to do.

7. I want to work for your company. Could I come in and meet with someone to talk about that? Anytime would be cool with me.

8. Hey. We just want to say a big "Thank You!" for all the stuff you gave our club for the spring play. You guys totally rock!

9. Please accept this letter of recommendation for Raul Porras. He is one of my best friends. Raul is responsible. He can be counted on to stay positive under pressure. He is also a professional and friendly employee. In fact, we count on him to welcome newcomers.

10. I am writing to request a copy of my last bill. I seem to have lost mine. I'm sorry about that.

For additional help, review pages 262–265 in your textbook or visit www.voyagesinenglish.com.

Chapter 2 • 135

Purpose, Audience, and Tone

A business letter should be written with the **purpose, audience,** and **tone** in mind. State your purpose early in the body and choose words appropriate for your audience and the tone you want to convey.

Write *application, request, gratitude,* or *complaint* to identify the purpose of each statement.

1. We would be grateful if you would consider visiting this fall. _____

2. Unfortunately, the product does not meet our expectations. _____

3. I greatly appreciate your service on the project. _____

4. My experience is uniquely suited to the demands of the job. _____

5. I believe my dedication to assisting elderly people makes me an excellent match for this position. _____

6. We found your simple gesture to be profoundly thoughtful. _____

7. Please think about donating a family pack of movie passes. _____

8. This kind of customer service is simply not acceptable. _____

Write an appropriate tone for each topic.

9.
Purpose: You are applying to be a lifeguard at a pool. You summarize your swimming ability and safety training.
Audience: Bill Mueller, the head lifeguard at the pool

Tone: _____

10.
Purpose: You are complaining to the manufacturer about a leaky hummingbird feeder. You describe when and where you bought the feeder and your experience in trying to use it.
Audience: a customer service representative

Tone: _____

11.
Purpose: You are asking your uncle to send you a copy of the science-fiction novel he wrote. You describe science-fiction novels you've read and liked before.
Audience: your favorite uncle

Tone: _____

For additional help, review pages 266–269 in your textbook or visit www.voyagesinenglish.com.

LESSON

3 Adjective Clauses

Adjective clauses modify a noun or a pronoun and usually begin with a relative pronoun. Adjective clauses can improve your writing by shifting the emphasis, deepening the meaning, or increasing the variety of sentences.

Underline each adjective clause.

1. My brother, who is 3 years older than I, turned 13 last weekend.

2. My parents, who are normally strict, allowed him to get a pet of his own.

3. My brother was the spelling bee winner, which made him proud.

4. Carl, whom my brother called to tell about the gift, came running over to our house.

5. Dad turned onto the road that goes past the school to get to the shelter.

6. The car, which needed a new battery, wouldn't start.

7. We got in the van, which is in much better condition, and set off for the shelter.

8. At the shelter it was lunchtime, which is why all the dogs were barking, when we arrived.

9. We talked to the director who is in charge of adoptions and offered our help.

10. Eventually the animals that were noisy became quiet, which was a relief.

11. My brother, who had fallen silent, was staring at a group of cats.

12. The cats that were in the first cage were mostly eating.

13. One cat that was gray and white was staring back at us.

14. It reached out a paw, which was tiny and fluffy, as though it was waving at us.

15. My brother named the cat Tiger, which is a great name for a cat, and we brought it home.

Complete each sentence with an adjective clause that shifts the emphasis, deepens the meaning, or adds variety.

16. Breakfast, _____, was a big meal.

17. His father, _____, was one of nine children.

18. I did not know you have a horse _____.

19. The team's mascot, _____, is called Clinky.

20. The man _____ is the one to ask.

On another sheet of paper, write three descriptive sentences. Use an adjective clause in each sentence.

For additional help, review pages 270–273 in your textbook or visit www.voyagesinenglish.com.

Roots

A **root** is the base from which a word is built. Looking for a root inside a word can help you understand its meaning.

Underline the root in each italicized word. Write the letter of the matching root meaning. Use a dictionary if you need help. Then think about what your response would be to each sentence.

1. Name two things you *transport* to school. _____ **a.** life

2. Name two things a jeweler might *inscribe* on a ring. _____ **b.** listen

3. Name two *aquatic* animals. _____ **c.** people

4. Name two things you study in *biology*. _____ **d.** carry

5. Name two sounds you might hear in an *auditorium*. _____ **e.** write

6. Name two events you have attended as a *spectator*. _____ **f.** watch

7. Name two *epidemics* that have happened in the past. _____ **g.** water

8. Name two things you might see at a *graduation*. _____ **h.** step

Use each root to help you find the appropriate word to complete each sentence.

flect: meaning "bend"

9. Amber noticed how the light _____ off the clean glass.

10. Somehow Audrey managed to _____ all the criticism and stay positive.

gram: meaning "letter" or "written"

11. The teacher's focus on _____ helped the class improve its writing over the year.

12. Eduardo decided to draw a _____ to better communicate the idea in his report.

migr: meaning "change" or "move"

13. Every winter the birds _____ to a warmer climate.

14. Many _____ to America work hard and hope to become productive citizens.

Study each word's root. Then write the meaning for each word on another sheet of paper. Use a dictionary as needed.

15. remiss	18. podium	21. sanitation
16. symphony	19. photogenic	22. query
17. infinite	20. advocate	23. appendix

© Loyola Press. Voyages in English Grade 7

For additional help, review pages 274–277 in your textbook or visit www.voyagesinenglish.com.

LESSON
5

Writing Tools

A **summary** is a condensed version of a text or other source, written in your own words. **Paraphrasing** is restating individual passages in a more detailed way than a summary. A **direct quotation** contains words identical to the original text.

Read each passage. Then identify the italicized text as a summary or a paraphrased piece and explain your answer.

1. **Passage:** Superman was the original comic-book superhero. At his inception in 1938, he was faster than a speeding bullet, more powerful than a locomotive, and could leap tall buildings in a single bound. However, he could not fly until 1941.

   Superman was introduced in 1938 with all the powers he has today, except he could not fly.

   _____

   _____

2. **Passage:** *The War of the Worlds* was a radio play based on a short story written by H.G. Wells. Many listeners who tuned into the show late missed the explanation that the radio show was fictional. They believed that the announcer and reporter in the show were real and that the events being reported, that Martians were invading Earth, were really happening.

   The War of the Worlds *is a short story by H.G. Wells about Martians invading Earth. It was turned into a radio play. Even though it was announced that the show was fictional, some listeners missed this part. They believed that the events were actually occurring.*

   _____

   _____

3. **Passage:** In 1945 Pennsylvania engineer Richard James was at home working with springs on a military invention. When he accidentally knocked one of the long, coiled springs off a bookshelf, he got the idea of marketing it as a toy instead. The inventor's wife, Betty, named the toy "Slinky." The Slinky has changed little since it was first introduced.

   A Pennsylvania engineer accidentally invented the Slinky in 1945 when he knocked a long, coiled spring off a bookshelf.

   _____

   _____

4. What are some similarities and differences between a summary and paraphrasing?

   _____

   _____

For additional help, review pages 278–281 in your textbook or visit www.voyagesinenglish.com.

Chapter 2 • 139

What Makes a Good How-to Article?

How-to writing is a kind of expository writing. How-to writing provides information that explains how to do or make something.

Read the article. Then answer the questions.

Feeling bored on a windy day? Then go fly a kite. The first thing you need to do is get a kite and a large ball of string. Read the directions that came with your kite to find out how to put it together and how to attach the string. Next, take your kite to a large, open area with no tree branches or overhead power lines. Determine which way the wind is blowing. Then hold your kite as high as you can so the wind can lift it. As the wind catches the kite, begin to let out your string. Then start walking backward to keep the string tight. If your kite is stable, let out more string to make it fly higher. When you are ready to go home, slowly wind up the string and bring down your kite.

1. What is the purpose of this how-to paragraph?

   _____

2. Why are the sentences written as steps?

   _____

   _____

3. What is the first step when you fly a kite?

   _____

4. What should you do after you find a large, open space?

   _____

5. Provide an example from the paragraph of a sentence in the imperative mood.

   _____

6. What materials or tools has the author specified?

   _____

7. This article might be found in a book about kites. Where else might you find how-to articles?

   _____

   _____

© Loyola Press. Voyages in English   Grade 7

For additional help, review pages 300–303 in your textbook or visit www.voyagesinenglish.com.

Relevant Details

Relevant details support the topic of a how-to article. A paragraph has unity when every detail relates to the topic sentence or main idea.

Choose a how-to topic from this list. Write the steps needed to complete the activity. If you have more than six steps, list them on another sheet of paper. Then complete the sentences that follow.

How to multiply two-digit numbers   How to upload a document

How to make your favorite snack   How to fix a flat tire

1.
Step 1

Step 2

Step 3

Step 4

Step 5

Step 6

2. My most explicit details are _____.

3. The intended audience is _____.

4. The relevant details are arranged in _____ order.

5. My article would be clearer if I _____.

On another sheet of paper, use your steps to write a how-to paragraph. Exchange papers with a partner and look for any misfit sentences.

© Loyola Press. Voyages in English Grade 7

For additional help, review pages 304–307 in your textbook
or visit www.voyagesinenglish.com.

Chapter 3 • 141

Transition Words

Transition words connect ideas in a logical order. These words help the details in a how-to article flow smoothly.

Use the transition words in the box to complete the sentences. Use a variety of words, but repeat some words if they make the most sense.

above	after	because	before	behind	but	consequently	finally
first	however	instead	later	next	now	therefore	soon
still	then	so	yet	last	under	in conclusion	again

1. Cream the mixture _____ adding butter, eggs, and sugar to the bowl.

2. Use cotton if available; _____, this pattern will work for silk as well.

3. _____, I hope I have convinced you that anyone can cook a great quiche.

4. Tussah silk has a different texture _____ the silkworms eat real leaves.

5. Knead the dough _____, this time for only five minutes.

6. _____, you can add a coat of clear varnish for durability.

7. _____, allow the bread to cool for 10 minutes before removing it from the pan.

8. _____ starting the engine, carefully adjust the choke.

9. Don't add the vanilla _____; wait until after the fudge is boiling rapidly.

10. _____, lay out your materials on the table so each is easy to grab.

11. Place the second paper cutout _____ the first one and glue together.

12. Pick up the second wrench _____, and use it to secure the bolts.

13. _____ congratulate yourself on assembling your very own laser pointer.

Choose one of the topics below. On another sheet of paper, write a how-to paragraph about your topic. Use at least five transition words in your paragraph.

A. You have developed a surefire strategy for earning high scores on a popular computer game. Write a paragraph that explains the first three steps in your strategy.

B. You want to make your favorite meal for dinner. Describe the first three steps you take to prepare the meal.

C. You are a guest instructor at a sports camp. It is your job to demonstrate how to perform a sports skill and teach a group of eight-year-olds how to perform it. Write a paragraph that explains the first three things you will do.

For additional help, review pages 308–311 in your textbook or visit www.voyagesinenglish.com.

LESSON 4

Adverb Clauses

An **adverb clause** usually modifies a verb, though it can also modify an adjective or another adverb. Adverb clauses are used to add variety or change the meaning of a sentence and are introduced by subordinate conjunctions.

Underline the adverb clauses. Circle the word or words each clause modifies.

1. The alarm went off because the exit door was opened.
2. If you make Jan a card, maybe she will help you with your homework.
3. Kyle has been arriving at school on time since he started jogging in the morning.
4. The puppy barked until the bearded man held out his hand.
5. After the mulberry bush was damaged, the gardener planted a new bush.
6. Put on your shoes before you stub your toe on the sidewalk.
7. So that everyone gets a turn, each person will speak for only five minutes.
8. We all can go on the field trip, provided everyone turns in a permission slip.

Revise each sentence pair by making one sentence an adverb clause.

9. My aunt introduced me to pickled okra. I don't know how I had lived without it.

   _____

10. Check the pan carefully for cracks. Pour the batter into the pan.

   _____

11. Don't try to start the engine. Reconnect the throttle cable.

   _____

12. You are attending the drama club meeting. You can bring the box of costumes.

   _____

13. They will harden as they cool. The cookies may appear raw in the middle.

   _____

Complete each sentence with an appropriate adverb clause.

14. While _____, the kitchen smelled like apples.
15. Her suitcase looked _____.
16. When _____, the dancers began their routine.
17. Call your parents if _____.
18. From the brush the lion watched the zebras until _____.

© Loyola Press. Voyages in English   Grade 7

For additional help, review pages 312–315 in your textbook or visit www.voyagesinenglish.com.

Dictionary

A **dictionary** contains an alphabetical list of words. For each word, the entry includes the definition, the syllabication, the part of speech, and the pronunciation.

Look up each italicized word in a dictionary. On another sheet of paper, write the definition that best fits the context of the sentence.

1. Michael *bristled* at the insinuation that he had cheated on the exam.

2. Suspecting a *bug*, the spy carefully dismantled the lamp to find the tiny wires.

3. We sorted the bills by their *denominations*.

4. They did everything to keep the flowers alive, but in the end the drought *prevailed*.

5. Our class staged a mock *summit* at the same time the world leaders were meeting.

6. The *tone* of the colors in the painting gave it a melancholy mood.

7. The president put Governor Rasband in charge of *affairs* of the state.

8. We were all encouraged to avoid *cheap* jokes in the talent show.

9. The family was a bit alarmed when Grandma decided to paint her bathroom a *deep* purple.

10. Don't *interfere* with the children's attempts to solve the problem on their own.

Find the meaning of each word. Write a sentence that illustrates its meaning.

11. feign _____

12. fiasco _____

Use the sample dictionary entry below to answer the questions that follow.

de • mean (di-**mēn**) *tr. v.* 1. To conduct or behave in a particular manner. [From Old French *demener*] 2. To lower, as in dignity or social standing: *The dog refused to demean herself by eating out of the trash.* [From English *mean*, to humble] **de • meaned, de • mean • ing, de • means**

13. What part of speech is *demean*? _____

14. How many syllables does *demean* have? _____

15. How many meanings does *demean* have? _____

On another sheet of paper, write two sentences using *demean*. Each sentence should demonstrate a different meaning.

© Loyola Press. Voyages in English   Grade 7

For additional help, review pages 316–319 in your textbook or visit www.voyagesinenglish.com.

LESSON
1

What Makes a Good Description?

Descriptive writing uses vivid vocabulary to portray a person, a place, or a thing. A good **description** will capture a reader's senses and imagination.

Complete each sentence with information about descriptive writing.

1. Descriptive writing gives the reader _____.

2. A good thing to do before writing a description is to picture _____ and consider _____.

3. Writing a description is like painting _____ for the reader.

4. In descriptive writing, the author sets a mood or creates _____.

5. _____ is a more vivid, exact word for *clean*.

6. _____ is a more vivid, exact word for *nice*.

7. _____ is an example of a word that appeals to the sense of touch.

8. _____ is an example of a word that appeals to the sense of sound.

Read each topic, picture the scene in your mind, and write three descriptive words you could use to describe the scene you visualized.

9. rainy night

_____ _____ _____

10. snowstorm

_____ _____ _____

11. walk on a windy day

_____ _____ _____

12. summer afternoon

_____ _____ _____

13. late autumn day

_____ _____ _____

Find an example of a descriptive paragraph. On another sheet of paper, answer the following questions about the paragraph.

14. What is the topic of the paragraph?

15. How did the writer help you visualize what was being described?

16. What was the mood of the description? List three words or phrases the writer used to convey the mood.

17. List two examples of words the writer used to appeal to the senses.

For additional help, review pages 338–341 in your textbook or visit www.voyagesinenglish.com.

Chapter 4 • **145**

LESSON 2

Organization

Organize details so that one detail flows logically into the next. Depending on your topic, you may want to use different kinds of organization such as **spatial order**, **chronological order**, and **comparing and contrasting**.

Write whether you would organize each topic by *spatial order*, by *chronological order*, or by *comparing and contrasting*.

1. how my new game is better than my old one   _____

2. the interior of the International Space Station   _____

3. a visit to Ralph Waldo Emerson's home   _____

4. a trip to Japan and China   _____

5. the characters Voldemort and Uncle Olaf   _____

6. a birthday celebration   _____

7. a family vacation   _____

8. a sales brochure for a recreational vehicle   _____

Write details on this Venn diagram comparing and contrasting life in the city to life in the country.

Living in the City
Larger population
_____
_____
_____
_____

Both
People live
and work
_____
_____
_____

Living in the Country
More open fields
_____
_____
_____
_____

On another sheet of paper, write five descriptive sentences comparing and contrasting life in the city to life in the country, using the ideas above.

For additional help, review pages 342–345 in your textbook or visit www.voyagesinenglish.com.

LESSON
3

Noun Clauses

A **noun clause** is a dependent clause used as a noun. A noun clause can be used as a subject, a subject complement, a direct object, an object of a preposition, and an appositive.

Underline the noun clause in each sentence. Write whether the noun clause is used as a *subject*, a *subject complement*, a *direct object*, an *object of a preposition*, or an *appositive*.

1. We do not know where the lost puppy lives.   _____

2. Please tell her how to get to the library.   _____

3. The best time is whenever you want it to be.   _____

4. Read the directions for what you should do next.   _____

5. What the baby needs is a warm blanket.   _____

6. Whoever swims the fastest will win the race.   _____

7. The idea that we can complete this in one night is ludicrous. _____

8. A coat of paint will restore the room to how it used to look. _____

9. I love how my dog makes me feel when I get home.   _____

10. The Baghetti brothers are whom you should call for help.   _____

11. Whichever soap you choose will do the job as well.   _____

12. The horses that she will drive are white.   _____

Use each set of words to write a sentence with a noun clause.

13. scientists believe, meteor may have caused climate changes

_____

14. everyone wondered, come through the door next

_____

15. bank will give a reward, supplies them with information about the robbery

_____

16. children are well prepared, seems obvious

_____

17. a sign of fitness, heart rate responds to brisk activity

_____

© Loyola Press. Voyages in English   Grade 7

For additional help, review pages 346–349 in your textbook
or visit www.voyagesinenglish.com.

Chapter 4 • 147

Adjective and Adverb Suffixes

A **suffix** can change the function, or use, of a word. Suffixes added to nouns or verbs can create adjectives, nouns, or adverbs. A suffix that creates an adjective is an **adjective suffix.** An **adverb suffix** creates an adverb.

Write a suffix to complete each sentence. Use a dictionary if needed.

1. We gasped, feeling the plan was exceptionally audac_____.

2. The cat's matern_____ instincts were obvious when she moved to protect the kitten.

3. We thought Norford was being a little self_____ not to share his art supplies.

4. Helen is the most act_____ of the six children.

5. Albert thoughtful_____ replaced the cap on the milk jug.

6. The scen_____ view from the cabin window enticed us to go outside.

7. The silk_____ texture of the fabric gave the dress an elegant appearance.

8. My brother virtuous_____ did not eat any of the leftover dessert.

9. We found the new computer program to be trouble_____ and hard to use.

10. The barber careful_____ cleaned and stored the razors and scissors.

Write a new word made by adding an adjective suffix to each base word.

11. tact	_____	17. nature	_____
12. vigil	_____	18. perish	_____
13. fame	_____	19. grace	_____
14. hero	_____	20. create	_____
15. negate	_____	21. differ	_____
16. bother	_____	22. peril	_____

Write a sentence using each base word and the suffix in parentheses.

23. pleasant (-*ly*)

_____

24. rebel (-*ious*)

_____

25. elude (-*ive*)

_____

© Loyola Press. Voyages in English   Grade 7

For additional help, review pages 350–353 in your textbook or visit www.voyagesinenglish.com.

Outlines

An **outline** is a plan for a piece of writing that helps you organize your ideas. An outline helps you focus each paragraph on one idea and makes sure that every detail in the paragraph supports that idea.

Complete each sentence by circling all the choices that are correct.

1. An outline is
   a. a plan for writing that helps you organize ideas.
   b. a tool to ensure each paragraph focuses on one idea and the details support that idea.
   c. a division of ideas that follows a specific format.
   d. an organizer that helps you compare and contrast your opinions.

2. To create an outline,
   a. begin by deciding on a main idea.
   b. use only complete sentences with correct punctuation and capitalization.
   c. label each main idea with a Roman numeral followed by a period.
   d. list subtopics under each main idea and the details under each subtopic.

3. Once an outline is created,
   a. it should not be rewritten or modified.
   b. it can help you see what ideas need further revision.
   c. check for balance to make sure items show equal importance.
   d. look for details that are out of place or do not belong.

Read the section of an outline and answer the questions.

I. Percy Jackson goes on a quest to redeem himself.
   A. has adventures and makes discoveries
      1. finds out his father is the god Poseidon
      2. best friend turns out to be a satyr sent to protect him
      3. may be kicked out of school for fighting a monster

4. What would you expect to come after this part of the outline?

_____

5. What is the subtopic? _____

6. What are the supporting details? _____

_____

For additional help, review pages 388–391 in your textbook or visit www.voyagesinenglish.com.

Chapter 5 • 153

Prefixes

A **prefix** is a syllable or syllables added to the beginning of a word. A prefix changes the meaning of the word to which it is added.

Underline the prefix in each word and write its meaning.

1. extraordinary _____
2. immature _____
3. transcribe _____

4. misanthrope _____
5. superimpose _____
6. preamble _____

7. incorrect _____
8. postscript _____
9. antifreeze _____

Write the word from the box to match each definition.

preclude	postdate	superhuman	incomplete	misspell
transpolar	antibody	interact	misfortune	indirect

10. not finished _____

11. something that acts against a virus _____

12. rule out in advance _____

13. write or say wrong letters _____

14. talk or act among one another _____

15. more than average person _____

16. bad luck _____

17. not going straight to the point _____

18. across the North or South Pole _____

19. to date something later than the real date _____

Add an appropriate prefix, using those found in the exercises above, to each word below. Then write a sentence using each new word.

20. cede _____

21. accurate _____

22. caution _____

23. bacterial _____

24. calculate _____

What Makes Good Fantasy Fiction?

Fantasy fiction takes readers to places they have never experienced. It has a beginning, a middle, and an end that provide an organized pattern of events and a clear line between good and evil.

Read each statement. Circle *T* if the statement is true or *F* if it is false.

1. Fantasy fiction is usually factual.   T   F

2. The setting of a fantasy story may be a different world.   T   F

3. The plot of a fantasy story is usually told out of sequence.   T   F

4. The problem or conflict is introduced toward the end.   T   F

5. The plot is usually developed in the middle of the fantasy story.   T   F

6. The series of spiraling events in fantasy fiction is called the climax.   T   F

7. The main character achieves his or her goal at the end of a fantasy story.   T   F

Write *C* if each passage introduces a character and *S* if it introduces the setting. Some passages may do both.

8. Hadley looked out at the rain-soaked scene from under the relative dryness of her home's doorway. The heavy mist that accompanied the rain this time of year meant she couldn't see far out over the sea, but she thought maybe those black dots might be something. Yes, she was sure they were moving. Her heart began to beat faster. Were those ships? _____

9. Chiara got unsteadily to her feet. What had happened? Where was everyone? She felt about to cry but took a deep breath and then held it for a few seconds. Pull yourself together, she told herself. She was in a kind of underground cave. Light filtered in from above. Did I fall from up there? she wondered. The thought lifted her spirits a bit. She congratulated herself on being tough enough to survive that kind of fall. Then she began to look around for handholds. She knew she needed to get out of the cave. _____

10. Cascading down the rocky slope were thousands of waterfalls, weaving in and out of each other like an ever-changing dance of light. The setting sun gave the water a shimmering glow so that the young elf wondered for a moment if there might be gold under the surface. _____

11. Claude felt uneasy when he saw the castle walls. He was to go in through the main entrance and ask for Lord Phillipe, but he was overwhelmed by the feeling that this was a trap. Instinctively, he put his hand over the pocket sewn into his coat. The message wasn't for Lord Phillipe, but for his daughter. Claude jumped off his horse and rolled in the dusty road. He unbraided the horse's tail and removed the brass decorations from the saddle and bridle, working methodically until there were no signs left of his life as a prince. _____

For additional help, review pages 414–417 in your textbook or visit www.voyagesinenglish.com.

Chapter 6   •   155

LESSON
2

Plot Development

A good fantasy story includes a problem for the main character to face, obstacles to overcome, the dramatic moment toward which the story builds, and a satisfying resolution.

Write a word to complete each statement about the plot of a fantasy.

1. The _____ comes after the problem is solved and ties up any loose ends.

2. After the hero rid the town of bothersome dragons, he discovered the real enemy was an evil wizard. This is a summary of the story's _____.

3. The _____ is the most dramatic moment of the story when the main character finally solves or faces his or her problem.

4. The main character may face many problems, but one is a fundamental issue that thwarts the hero from accomplishing his or her goals. This is called the story's _____.

Identify the conflict and resolution in each summary of a fantasy story.

Nima lives on a desert planet where widely scattered oases are the only support for a group of colonies. A new virus sweeps through her colony, so Nima and her friends set out to find help. One friend falls ill, but Nima finds the cure. Unfortunately, a sandstorm destroys the vehicle in which they were traveling, so Nima uses her wits to return in time to save lives.

5. Conflict: _____

_____

6. Resolution: _____

_____

Umi and Oni are royalty in an ancient African kingdom when they stumble across a way to travel forward in time. Umi searches desperately for a way to get home again, but Oni quickly adapts to modern life and doesn't want to return. Umi learns to make peace with the fact that this is her brother's decision, and Oni comes to see how his sister can take what she learned in the present and use it to improve the past. When they do find the way home, they return united and wiser.

7. Conflict: _____

_____

8. Resolution: _____

_____

© Loyola Press. Voyages in English **Grade 7**

For additional help, review pages 418–421 in your textbook or visit www.voyagesinenglish.com.

Dialogue

Dialogue adds interest to a scene by helping readers feel that they are right in the middle of the action. Dialogue is also an effective way of conveying emotion, humor, and subtle information about the characters.

Write nine words that can replace the word *said* and help describe the manner in which a character speaks.

1. _____   4. _____   7. _____

2. _____   5. _____   8. _____

3. _____   6. _____   9. _____

Read the dialogue and answer the questions.

"Miguel and Tam, sitting in a tree," sang Elena in a singsong voice.
"Stop!" Miguel yelled, and then more softly he continued, "that's not funny, Elena. Tam is my friend and she's very sick."
Elena looked surprised. "It's not—, I didn't mean—," she stammered, growing red-faced. Finally, she sighed, "I'm sorry, Miguel."

10. Which character is probably younger? Why? _____
_____

11. How does the author use dialogue to show that the characters know each other well?
_____
_____

Add punctuation to the dialogue for the first character. Then write a response of dialogue for the second character.

12. Description: two children flying on an airplane for the first time

Look at how small the houses seem squealed Bridget

_____

13. Description: a paramedic helping a man in a car accident

Do you think my leg is broken Jonathan cried

_____

14. Description: a comic-book hero confronting a villain

So hissed the evildoer you think you can foil my diabolical plan do you

_____

For additional help, review pages 422–425 in your textbook or visit www.voyagesinenglish.com.

Chapter 6 • 157

LESSON
4

Figurative Language

Figurative language compares one thing to another in a way that adds interest and insight to the comparison.

Complete each sentence with the figure of speech in parentheses.

1. The tumbleweeds _____. (personification)

2. This pile of dirty clothes is _____. (hyperbole)

3. The baby's skin is _____. (simile)

4. Our new house is _____. (metaphor)

5. The flowers _____ in the breeze. (personification)

6. During the summer, the gym is _____. (simile)

7. That final exam was _____. (metaphor)

8. The chair _____ under the man's weight. (personification)

9. It's so cold today that _____. (hyperbole)

10. After the triathlon, my body _____. (simile)

11. My brother's old clunker of a car was _____. (metaphor)

Rewrite each sentence by replacing the underlined cliché with more effective figurative language.

12. We tried to eat the bread rolls, but they were hard as rocks.

_____

13. The interior of the apple was as white as snow.

_____

14. The look in her eyes was as cold as ice.

_____

15. The mighty castle was as old as the earth itself.

_____

16. Hurrying here and there, the stonemason was as busy as a beaver.

_____

For additional help, review pages 426–429 in your textbook or visit www.voyagesinenglish.com.

Limericks

The structure of a **limerick** follows exact rules, but the result is fun and easy to remember.

Circle the letter of the choice that correctly completes each statement.

1. Limericks are best described as
   a. poems that tell sad stories.
   b. poems about nature.
   c. silly rhymes that tell stories.
   d. real-life narratives.

2. Limericks usually feature all the following except
   a. fantastic characters.
   b. real people.
   c. surprising situations.
   d. humorous conclusions.

3. Limericks are probably a commonly used poetic form because they are
   a. easy to write.
   b. short, fun, and easy to remember.
   c. based on true stories.
   d. stories with a moral.

4. To write a limerick, a poet might use
   a. an atlas.
   b. an encyclopedia.
   c. a dictionary.
   d. a rhyming dictionary.

Use syllable stress marks to identify the stressed and unstressed syllables in each line. Circle the line if it contains an example of anapestic rhythm.

5. There was an odd, damp odor.

6. She liked to collect ants.

7. "Won't you live in my shoe?"

8. Every day they bought oranges.

9. Each morning at dawn.

10. He robbed the young man of defeat.

Underline the word that does not rhyme in each set and replace it with a word that does.

11. screwdriver, conniver, survivor, quiver   _____

12. bombastic, postmaster, gymnastic, elastic   _____

13. brother, our, power, shower   _____

14. chore, order, floor, oar   _____

15. quicker, heretic, lunatic, dirty trick   _____

What Makes Good Expository Writing?

Expository writing provides factual information. Its purpose is to inform, explain, or define something to its audience. One kind of expository writing is the expository article.

Answer the questions.

1. What should a reader expect to learn from an expository article?

   _____

   _____

2. What should be included in the introduction of an expository article?

   _____

   _____

3. How are the subtopics often organized in the body of an expository article?

   _____

   _____

4. Should the writer include mostly facts or opinions in an expository article? Why?

   _____

   _____

5. What is the purpose of the conclusion of an expository article?

   _____

   _____

6. How do the details for an expository article differ from its main idea?

   _____

   _____

7. How might a writer gather details to support the main idea?

   _____

   _____

8. What may cause a writer's main idea to change as he or she gathers details?

   _____

   _____

For additional help, review pages 452–455 in your textbook or visit www.voyagesinenglish.com.

LESSON
2

Fact and Opinion

Facts are statements that can be proved true or false. **Opinions** are statements that tell what someone believes. In an expository article, opinions should be avoided unless they are those of experts.

Write *fact* or *opinion* to identify each statement. Circle the opinion signal words.

1. The American tree sparrow is common to Alaska and northern Canada. _____

2. The amazing physicist Gwyn Jones used motorcycle parts in her work. _____

3. In 1794 Eli Whitney patented the cotton gin. _____

4. Women give chocolate to men on Valentine's Day in Japan. _____

5. In a charming return, men give women gifts a month later on White Day. _____

6. A tractor-drawn aerial is a fascinating type of fire truck that has a separate steering mechanism for the rear wheels. _____

7. Concerns over security have triggered proposed legislation requiring online sites with photographic maps to blur out public buildings. _____

8. The Akashi-Kaikyo Bridge is the world's longest suspension bridge. _____

Write one fact and one opinion about each topic.

9. an occupation

Fact: _____

Opinion: _____

10. a recent school event

Fact: _____

Opinion: _____

11. an animal kept as a pet

Fact: _____

Opinion: _____

Cross out the statement that is least relevant to an essay about a mosquito control program.

12. There are approximately 3,500 species of mosquitoes.

13. Mosquitoes are the most deadly disease carriers known, killing millions of people each year.

14. Mosquitoes go through four stages in their life cycle: egg, larva, pupa, and adult.

15. Mosquitoes lay their eggs near open sources of water.

For additional help, review pages 456–459 in your textbook
or visit www.voyagesinenglish.com.

Noun and Verb Suffixes

A **suffix** is a syllable or syllables added to the end of a word to change its meaning. Suffixes may create nouns or verbs when added to other words.

Complete each sentence by adding a noun suffix to the word in parentheses.

1. The boxes in the _____ need to be labeled and stacked. (base)

2. For your own _____, please be sure your seatbelt is securely fastened. (safe)

3. After living in Iowa for most of her life, Liz is now a _____ of Arizona. (reside)

4. The enthusiastic audience gave a standing ovation to the _____. (piano)

5. Because the hotel had no _____, we had to keep driving. (vacant)

6. Their _____ has endured over the years. (friend)

7. The woman peered through the _____ as she tried to locate the light switch. (dark)

8. Joan valued her job as the _____ to the foundation's president. (assist)

9. By claiming an _____, Randolph received a substantial tax refund. (exempt)

10. Miles suddenly became aware of the _____ of his situation. (real)

Write a new word by adding a verb suffix to each word. Then write a sentence for the new word.

11. soft _____

_____

12. active _____

_____

13. computer _____

_____

14. terror _____

_____

15. less _____

_____

16. real _____

_____

© Loyola Press. Voyages in English   Grade 7

For additional help, review pages 460–463 in your textbook or visit www.voyagesinenglish.com.

Quotations

Direct quotations are a person's exact words, either spoken or in print, that are incorporated into your own writing.

Circle the number of each sentence that is correct. Add the correct punctuation and capitalization to the sentences that are incorrect.

1. I regret that I have but one life to give for my country wrote Nathan Hale.

2. Socrates believed that "wisdom begins in wonder."

3. The teacher said Explain the proverb The road to a friend's house is never long.

4. "Where there is love there is life," said Mahatma Gandhi.

5. Ralph Waldo Emerson said People only see what they are prepared to see.

6. Quinn asked me what Francis Bacon meant when he said, "Knowledge is power."

7. If you judge people, you have no time to love them Mother Teresa proclaimed.

8. My father likes this quotation by Mark Twain: "You cannot depend on your eyes when your imagination is out of focus."

9. You're happiest while you're making the greatest contribution, said Robert F. Kennedy.

10. The future declared Eleanor Roosevelt belongs to those who believe in the beauty of their dreams.

11. My instructor said, When I start to worry, I remember Nichiren Daishonin's words: No one can avoid problems, not even saints or sages

Write a sentence using each direct quotation.

12. Hope is the dream of a man awake. —French Proverb

_____

13. He who has imagination without learning has wings and no feet. —Joseph Joubert

_____

14. A friend is one who knows you and loves you just the same. —Elbert Hubbard

_____

15. A person who never made a mistake never tried anything new. —Albert Einstein

_____

16. Happiness depends upon ourselves. —Aristotle

_____

© Loyola Press. Voyages in English   Grade 7

For additional help, review pages 464–467 in your textbook or visit www.voyagesinenglish.com.

Library and Internet Sources

When researching information, two of the most efficient ways of finding information are to use references from the **library and Internet sources.**

Write the letter to match each library reference or Internet source to its description.

1. _____ a periodical
2. _____ *Reader's Guide*
3. _____ a .org site
4. _____ an atlas
5. _____ a .com site
6. _____ an encyclopedia
7. _____ a .edu site
8. _____ an almanac or a yearbook
9. _____ a .mil site
10. _____ a .gov site

a. a website developed by an organization
b. something published at regular intervals
c. articles on specific topics arranged alphabetically
d. maps and other geographic information
e. listings of magazine articles
f. a military website
g. a government website
h. a commercial website
i. a website developed by a school
j. annual facts, statistics, and news items

Circle the letters of the two websites that would likely provide the most reliable information for each topic.

11. the number of congressional state representatives for Massachusetts
    a. a .gov site for the U.S. Congress
    b. a .com site with educational games
    c. a .gov site with congressional maps
    d. a .org site for Massachusetts history

12. the meaning and etymology of a word
    a. a .edu site from a prominent university
    b. a .com site of a respected print dictionary
    c. a .com dictionary with numerous ads
    d. a .com site to which anyone can contribute articles or information

13. the life of President Lincoln
    a. a .gov site about Georgia history
    b. a .com site selling books about Lincoln
    c. a .gov site about former U.S. presidents
    d. a .org site about American presidents

List three library resources you could use to research the topic. Then list three keywords you might use to find information on the Internet.

Topic: the history of the Alamo

Resources: _____

Keywords: _____

For additional help, review pages 468–471 in your textbook or visit www.voyagesinenglish.com.

LESSON
1

What Makes a Good Research Report?

A **research report** explores a specific idea about a topic. Facts are gathered by researching sources such as interviews, books, encyclopedias, almanacs, magazines, newspapers, maps, and documents on the Internet.

Circle the letter of the answer that correctly completes each sentence.

1. The purpose of a research report is to
   a. entertain.
   b. inform.
   c. explain how to do something.

2. The tone of a research report is
   a. formal.
   b. informal.
   c. humorous.

3. A Works Cited page lists
   a. topics.
   b. details.
   c. sources.

4. A thesis statement presents the
   a. main idea.
   b. sources used.
   c. conclusion.

5. Details that support the thesis statement are grouped into
   a. graphics.
   b. subtopics.
   c. topics.

6. Information in a research report should
   a. come from friends.
   b. be in a table of contents.
   c. have several sources.

Read each thesis statement and write two kinds of sources that may provide information for the thesis.

7. Zwickau, Germany, is both an ancient city and a modern one.

_____

8. Yesterday the new library in our town was dedicated, making it easier for more people to gain free access to books and research materials.

_____

9. What could be a more worthwhile way to spend your spring break than by helping build affordable housing?

_____

10. The development of agriculture led to significant changes in human behavior.

_____

For additional help, review pages 490–493 in your textbook or visit www.voyagesinenglish.com.

Chapter 8 • 165

LESSON 2

Gathering and Organizing Information

Using note cards is one way to **gather and organize information.** Write on the note cards important details that relate to your topic. At the bottom of the card, write the source and page number.

Complete a note card listing at least three facts for each passage.

The Republic of Indonesia is a country that spans the Asian and Australian continents. It is made up of 17,508 islands, although only 6,000 of those islands are inhabited. Indonesia has a populaton of 237 million people. Only three other countries have more people: China, India, and the United States. Indonesia has an elected legislature and a president. Indonesia has a diverse collection of ethnic, linguistic, and religious groups.

—Indonesia by Heather Juno, page 115

The Asian, or Asiatic, elephant is one of the three living elephant species. These are the largest living land animals in Asia and are considered endangered. Asian elephants are often domesticated for use in forestry, tourism, and special occasions and ceremonies. Asian elephants are smaller than African elephants. They can be distinguished by their smaller ears and more slightly rounded back. The tip of their trunk has only one finger-like muscle instead of two.

—Walking Thunder by Steve Smith, page 18

For additional help, review pages 494–497 in your textbook or visit www.voyagesinenglish.com.

© Loyola Press. Voyages in English   Grade 7

© Loyola Press. Voyages in English   Grade 7

LESSON

3

Citing Sources

By **citing your sources** for the reader, you give credit to the source of each fact, idea, or quotation you find. It also tells the reader where to look for more information on the topic.

Write the type of information that is missing from each citation.

1. **Book:**

   Coville, Jayne. *Cooking with French Chefs*. Baton Rouge, LA: _____, 2001. Print.

2. **Encyclopedia:**

   _____. *The Encyclopaedia Britannica*. 2010 edition. Print.

3. **Website:**

   Sciacca, Mark. "Antique Cars." 2 Dec. 2009. Web. 13 Aug. 2016. _____.

Write *encyclopedia, book,* or *website* to identify the source of each citation.

4. "Jane Austen." *World Book*. 2010 edition. Print.   _____

5. Macaulay, David. *Castle*. New York, NY: Houghton Mifflin, 1977. Print. _____

6. "Branches of Government." 25 Mar. 2009. Web. 10 Nov. 2016.
   <http://bensguide.gpo.gov/6-8/government/branches.html>.   _____

7. "The Great Salt Lake." *New Book of Knowledge*. 2008 edition. Print. _____

8. Symes, Dr. R. F. and Dr. R. R. Harding. *Crystal and Gem*.
   New York, NY: DK Publishing, 1991. Print.   _____

9. King, Jr., Martin Luther. "Why I Am Opposed to the War in Vietnam."
   16 Apr. 1967. Web. 07 Sept. 2016.
   <http://www.hpol.org/record.php?id=150>.   _____

10. "Ankle Injuries." *Encyclopedia of Medicine*. 2004 edition. Print. _____

Circle the letter of the choice that best completes each statement.

11. Parenthetical notation is
    a. identifying which source a fact comes from.   **c.** identifying the website.
    b. identifying the type of source.   **d.** identifying the thesis of the report.

12. Plagiarism is
    a. listing the sources in the wrong order.   **c.** using someone's ideas as your own.
    b. including facts that don't support the topic.   **d.** using parenthetical notation.

Varied Sentences

Variety is one key to crafting engaging writing with an original voice. Create variety by changing the length, the type, and the structure of your sentences.

Write *natural* or *inverted* to indicate the order of each sentence. Then rewrite the sentence in the opposite order.

1. Above the ocean soared several seagulls.   _____

_____

2. The angry bull paced around the circular corral.   _____

_____

3. Hovering over her young is the mother deer.   _____

_____

4. On the hill overlooking the farm are packs of coyotes.   _____

_____

5. Racing through the streets were throngs of runners.   _____

_____

Rewrite each sentence as either interrogative or exclamatory. Modify the structure and add or change words if needed.

6. Students will begin the spring-cleanup campaign on Monday.

_____

7. The fireworks finale continued for five minutes uninterrupted.

_____

Rewrite each sentence to begin with a modifier.

8. Jan lifted the boulder with the help of her brother.

_____

9. The city streets look like a spider web on the map.

_____

10. The tiger crouched in its cage waiting for food.

_____

For additional help, review pages 502–505 in your textbook or visit www.voyagesinenglish.com.

Denotation and Connotation

A word's **denotation** is its dictionary definition. A word's **connotation** is the implied meaning of the word. Often it suggests a positive or negative value to a word.

Complete the chart by writing an appropriate word. Use a dictionary or thesaurus if you need help.

POSITIVE CONNOTATION	NEGATIVE CONNOTATION	DENOTATION
1. anticipation		expectation
2. lingers	loiters	
3.	nag	horse
4. moist		damp
5. scent		smell
6. converse	chatter	
7.	cowardly	shy
8.	pester	annoy

Rewrite each sentence using neutral words more appropriate for a research report.

9. The Cardinals' efforts fell short of the mark, and the Cubs won 6–3.

_____

10. The new mall will require destroying more than 85 homes in the area.

_____

11. The unproven governor had to make difficult decisions only two weeks into his term.

_____

12. Individuals who gambled in the stock market found themselves suddenly with little to no retirement funds.

_____

_____

13. Gaunt models teetered on spindly shoes as they careened down the walkway.

_____

_____

For additional help, review pages 506–509 in your textbook or visit www.voyagesinenglish.com.

© Loyola Press. Voyages in English Grade 7

Chapter 8 • 169

What Makes Good Argumentative Writing?

Argumentative writing is writing that makes a case for the validity of a claim about an arguable topic, using reasons and evidence.

Mark an X next to items that state a valid claim about an arguable topic.

1. Yesterday was the happiest day of my life.   _____

2. The voting age should be lowered.   _____

3. It is easy to build a tree fort.   _____

4. Walking through the forest on a rainy day is relaxing.   _____

5. Ivy League colleges should provide free tuition.   _____

**Write _T_ if the statement about argumentative essays is true.
Write _F_ if the statement is false.**

6. The introduction should state an arguable claim.   _____

7. Each support paragraph should offer a reason and evidence for the claim. _____

8. Counterclaims should be acknowledged and refuted.   _____

9. The conclusion should show a reader why the claim is logical.   _____

10. The tone should be casual and friendly.   _____

Imagine you are writing an argumentative essay claiming that your city should protect marshland near your home as a nature conservation area. Underline the reasons that should be included.

11. provides habitat for wildlife

12. protects an important ecological area

13. you like the open space

14. good place for your dog to run

15. preserves the area for future generations to enjoy

Write two additional reasons for protecting the marshland.

16. _____

17. _____

© Loyola Press. Voyages in English Grade 7

For additional help, review pages 530–533 in your textbook or visit www.voyagesinenglish.com.

Claim and Counterclaim

An effective argumentative essay includes a **claim** and a **counterclaim.** The claim states the arguable idea. The counterclaim acknowledges a different point of view.

Write *OK* for strong claims. Rewrite weak claims to make them strong.

1. Community service should be a mandatory school requirement.

    _____

2. All schools should require students to wear uniforms.

    _____

3. Taking vitamins is just as good as eating a balanced diet.

    _____

4. I love sports; playing sports should be a school requirement.

    _____

Circle the counterclaim in each pair of sentences.

5. The speed limit in our town should be increased to 65 mph.

    Some people say increasing the speed limit will cause accidents.

6. Educators often claim that more homework equals greater academic success.

    Homework should be limited to 30 minutes per night.

7. All beaches and lakes should be open to the public.

    Many homeowners think that their property includes adjacent beachfront and water.

8. Parents might think that children are drawn to plastic equipment and bright colors.

    Traditional playgrounds should be turned into natural playgrounds.

Read the following support paragraph. Identify the claim (*C*), support for claim (*S*), counterclaim (*CC*), and refutation (*R*).

All college students should hold part-time jobs. _____ Research shows that young adults who work are more likely to learn skills that their jobless counterparts do not. _____ Some people argue that students have plenty of time after college to work. _____ However, studies show that college graduates who have job experience are more likely to be hired. _____

For additional help, review pages 534–537 in your textbook or visit www.voyagesinenglish.com.

LESSON 3 Cause and Effect

A **cause-and-effect** argument makes a case for why something happened the way it did. There are several types of causal arguments: multiple causes, one effect; one cause, multiple effects; and chain, or domino, effect.

Match each cause to its possible effect.

1. oversleep _____ **a.** maintain a healthy weight

2. careful diet and exercise _____ **b.** late for an appointment

3. graduate from college _____ **c.** save trees

4. buy items with minimal packaging _____ **d.** more opportunity

5. practice volleyball _____ **e.** increase skills

Write one positive effect and one negative effect for each cause.

6. discovery of penicillin _____

_____

7. use of social media _____

_____

8. exploration of space _____

_____

9. invention of self-driving cars _____

_____

10. creation of the Internet _____

_____

Place the sentences in numbered order to create a cause-and-effect chain.

11. Water, dirt, and debris give way. _____

12. Heavy rains drench the ground. _____

13. Water collects on the land. _____

14. A landslide occurs. _____

15. Logging practices cause deforestation of land. _____

For additional help, review pages 538–541 in your textbook or visit www.voyagesinenglish.com.

Use Precise Language

Using **precise language** reflects thorough knowledge of a subject and helps a writer communicate facts and ideas in a clear, focused way. Domain-specific vocabulary is a type of precise language that includes terms or phrases used in a special setting, or domain.

Circle the letter of the sentence that provides more precise language.

1. **a.** Families who eat dinner together talk more and have stronger relationships.
   b. Eating together as a family is better.

2. **a.** People who have pets are happier.
   b. Caring for a pet can lead to better health, less stress, and a happier life.

Rewrite each sentence using precise language.

3. The children were glad to have a snow day. _____

_____

4. That tree in the park provided shade. _____

_____

5. The boy and girl counted their points after the game. _____

_____

Underline the domain-specific vocabulary in the paragraph. Then write synonyms for each word on the lines below.

We read the verdict of the trial in the newspaper. It was an open-and-shut case. The judgment was for the plaintiff. The defendant was charged with gross negligence. The plaintiff was awarded restitution.

6. _____

7. _____

8. _____

9. _____

10. _____

11. _____

12. _____

For additional help, review pages 542–545 in your textbook or visit www.voyagesinenglish.com.

Chapter 9 • 173

Digital References

Digital references, such as online dictionaries, glossaries, and thesauruses, help writers choose a precise word or verify a word's meaning.

What type of information would you expect to find offered for each digital reference?

1. pronunciation icon _____

2. hyperlink feature _____

3. online glossary _____

4. search bar _____

5. online thesaurus _____

Use an online thesaurus to find a synonym for each word listed below.

6. inhabitant _____

7. gasp _____

8. warm _____

9. happy _____

10. confident _____

Underline the domain-specific words in the paragraph. Look up these words in a subject-specific online glossary and write their meaning.

> Mari, perched on a stand-up paddleboard, was nervous as she paddled onto the lake. The leash and deck pad beneath her feet offered safety as she tried to balance the board. Double fins provided stability, but the board still felt wobbly. Suddenly, her foot slipped and touched the rail. Mari calmly righted herself to improve her tracking. Taking a deep breath, she touched blade to water and began again.

11. _____

12. _____

13. _____

14. _____

15. _____

16. _____

For additional help, review pages 546–549 in your textbook or visit www.voyagesinenglish.com

What Makes a Good Literary Analysis?

A **literary analysis** is an in-depth study of a piece of literature that discusses and evaluates the elements and techniques in a literary work.

Read each sentence. Identify each sentence that could be included in a literary analysis (*LA*).

1. In *Dark Sun*, the author uses setting to transport the reader to another place and time. _____

2. The author of *Golden Horse* shows us how nature can be more important than nurture. _____

3. I really enjoyed *A Different Kind of Summer*. _____

4. *Tomorrow* is a book about a boy and his dog. _____

5. Imagery is everywhere in *Nine Lives*, and the author plays to our senses deliberately. _____

Read each idea below. Mark with an *X* if it describes something that belongs in an introduction to a literary analysis.

6. your personal memories _____

7. the main claim that you want to make about the book _____

8. whether you liked or disliked the work _____

9. the author and title of the work _____

10. a brief explanation about the work _____

Think about a book you've read and a claim you would like to make about it. Write a topic sentence, a sentence that provides supporting details, and a conclusion sentence.

11. topic sentence: _____

_____

12. supporting details sentence: _____

_____

13. conclusion sentence: _____

_____

For additional help, review pages 568–571 in your textbook or visit www.voyagesinenglish.com.

Chapter 10 • 175

Analyzing Historical Fiction

LESSON 2

Historical fiction is a literary genre in which a fictional plot takes place in a period from the past. Analyzing historical fiction can reveal something about a historical event or time.

Write the letter to match the character type.

1. minor character _____   **a.** a character that changes in an important way
2. static character _____   **b.** a character or force that opposes
3. protagonist _____   **c.** a character that provides support
4. antagonist _____   **d.** a character that remains the same
5. dynamic character _____   **e.** a character the story revolves around

Write which part of a story's plot is described.

6. the necessary background needed to understand the story   _____
7. highest point of interest in the story   _____
8. the end of the falling action and conclusion to the story   _____

Read the following excerpt from a historical novel set on Prince Edward Island in Canada in the late 1800s. Then answer the questions.

That bridge led Anne's dancing feet up over a wooded hill beyond, where perpetual twilight reigned under the straight, thick-growing firs and spruces; the only flowers there were myriads of delicate "June bells," those shyest and sweetest of woodland blooms, and a few pale, aerial starflowers, like the spirits of last year's blossoms. Gossamers glimmered like threads of silver among the trees and the fir boughs and tassels seemed to utter friendly speech.

Excerpt from *Anne of Green Gables* by Lucy Maud Montgomery

9. What is the point of view? _____
10. What are three examples of imagery? _____

_____

11. What is an example of simile? _____
12. What is an example of personification? _____

_____

For additional help, review pages 572–575 in your textbook or visit www.voyagesinenglish.com.

Placing Modifiers Correctly

Modifiers add detail to sentences and can function as adjectives or adverbs. Place them close to the word being modified to avoid *misplaced*, *dangling*, and *squinting* modifiers.

Identify with an X each sentence that contains a dangling modifier.

1. Relaxing on the couch, Molly snoozed after an exhausting day.   _____

2. Sprinting quickly, his shirt caught on a tree branch.   _____

3. Cold and biting, the winter wind ripped through the village.   _____

4. Ready for the beach, my bags were packed and my sunglasses were on.   _____

Rewrite each sentence to correct the misplaced or dangling modifier.

5. Flying across the sky, Nora spotted a jet.

   _____

6. Sipping a cup of tea, my cat sat beside me.

   _____

7. Sophie gulped the water after practice that was cold.

   _____

8. Soaring over other tall buildings, Wyatt located Willis Tower.

   _____

Underline the squinting modifier. Then rewrite the sentence to make the meaning clear.

9. We take our family trip to the mountains always in July.

   _____

10. My dad awakens to bike early to the coffee shop.

    _____

11. Mrs. Rey announced that the quiz suddenly would be tomorrow.

    _____

12. Thad said after lunch he would drive home.

    _____

© Loyola Press. Voyages in English   **Grade 7**

For additional help, review pages 576–579 in your textbook or visit www.voyagesinenglish.com.

Chapter 10 • 177

Context Clues

When we are unsure of the meaning of a word, we can look for **context clues** surrounding the unknown word. Words, sentences, and word relationships can help uncover the meaning.

Use context clues in the sentence to guess the meaning of the underlined word.

1. When we saw the opossum eating both a mouse and an apple, we realized it was an <u>omnivore</u>.

   _____

2. Ben could not concentrate during the test because the construction noise was <u>perturbing</u> him.

   _____

3. My front yard is <u>convex</u> because the septic tank buried in the ground forms a mound.

   _____

4. Tory was surprised to find that the tadpoles' tails had disappeared and that she now had <u>froglets</u>.

   _____

Read the following passage. Use context clues to determine the meaning of the underlined words.

> I was twenty-seven years old when I <u>engaged</u> in the Underground Rail Road business, and I continued therein <u>diligently</u> until the breaking up of that business by the Great Rebellion. I then came to South Carolina to witness the <u>uprising</u> of a nation of slaves into the dignity and privileges of mankind.
>
> Excerpt from a letter by John Hunn in *The Underground Railroad* by William Still

5. engaged _____

6. diligently _____

7. uprising _____

Write a word to complete the second pair of words in each analogy.

8. bark : dog :: hoot : _____

9. saw : carpenter :: gavel : _____

10. New York : United States :: London : _____

© Loyola Press. Voyages in English **Grade 7**

For additional help, review pages 580–583 in your textbook or visit www.voyagesinenglish.com.

Figures of Speech

A **figure of speech** is a phrase used in an unusual, imaginative way to express ideas. An **allusion**—a reference to a well-known person, character, literary work, or event—is a type of figure of speech.

Identify the allusion in each sentence. Label it *literary*, *biblical*, or *mythological*.

1. The team embarked on an odyssey to locate the sports equipment.

   _____

2. I knew he was interested in horticulture, but he's truly a Johnny Appleseed!

   _____

3. Our class lined up for ice cream as if heeding the call of the Sirens.

   _____

4. When Mika fell in the street, she was thankful for the good Samaritan who helped her.

   _____

5. Henry likes to think he's a real Romeo, but he's not.

   _____

Read the explanation of each allusion. Then write a sentence using it correctly.

6. Cowardly Lion (literary allusion; refers to the fearful African lion character in *The Wonderful Wizard of Oz*)

   _____

   _____

7. Midas (mythological allusion; refers to a greedy king of Phrygia who wished that all he touched turned to gold)

   _____

   _____

Write three sentences, one using a biblical allusion, one using a mythological allusion, and one using a literary allusion. Write your sentences on another sheet of paper.

For additional help, review pages 584–587 in your textbook or visit www.voyagesinenglish.com.

What Makes a Good Sonnet?

A **sonnet** is a type of poetry that originated in Italy centuries ago. Sonnets focus on a single thought or idea. Structure is important in a good sonnet.

Complete each phrase to describe the quality of a sonnet.

rhyme scheme	a single thought or idea	14 lines	10 syllables

1. A sonnet has _____.

2. A sonnet has a specific _____.

3. Each sonnet ends with _____.

4. Each line contains _____.

Read Shakespeare's "Sonnet XII" and answer the questions below.

"Sonnet XII" by William Shakespeare

When I do count the clock that tells the time,   _____ _____

And see the brave day sunk in hideous night;   _____ _____

When I behold the violet past prime,   _____ _____

And sable curls, all silvered o'er with white;   _____ _____

When lofty trees I see barren of leaves,   _____ _____

Which erst from heat did canopy the herd,   _____ _____

And summer's green all girded up in sheaves   _____ _____

Borne on the bier with white and bristly beard: _____ _____

Then of thy beauty do I question make   _____ _____

That thou among the wastes of time must go,   _____ _____

Since sweets and beauties do themselves forsake,   _____ _____

And die as fast as they see others grow;   _____ _____

And nothing 'gainst time's scythe can make defence   _____ _____

Save breed to brave him when he takes thee hence.   _____ _____

5. In the left column, label the three quatrains using *Q1, Q2, Q3*. Label the couplet *C*.

6. In the right column, label the rhyme scheme with a letter for each line.

For additional help, review pages 606–609 in your textbook or visit www.voyagesinenglish.com.

LESSON
2

How to Write a Sonnet

Writing a sonnet requires attention to lines, rhyme, syllables, and meter. Follow these steps: **brainstorm topics, narrow ideas, choose the rhyme scheme, write,** and **sum up the sonnet.**

Narrow down three specific ideas for each broad topic.

1. my favorite restaurant: _____
   _____

2. the best dinner: _____
   _____

3. a dream: _____
   _____

4. my friend: _____
   _____

5. my love of music: _____
   _____

Write a quatrain about a favorite meal. Use an *ABAB* rhyme scheme.

6. _____
   _____
   _____
   _____

A sonnet ends with a couplet. Place an X next to the ideas that describe a couplet.

7. sums up ideas   _____

8. describes characters   _____

9. sometimes uses humor   _____

10. makes the sonnet memorable _____

11. rhymes   _____

12. presents an argument   _____

Using Commas Correctly

Commas are important and practical. They indicate a pause between parts of a sentence and separate items on a list. Commas prevent incorrect interpretations.

Read each sentence. Add a comma to set off the introductory word or words.

1. No I don't want to come to your cat's birthday party.

2. Luke and Maya would you like to go?

3. Unfortunately everyone seems busy.

4. Okay I guess it is short notice.

5. Well next year is his golden birthday anyway.

Read each sentence. Use commas to separate nouns in a series.

6. Mia Kate and Will are on the swim team.

7. The recipe calls for two eggs one cup of sugar and two cups of flour.

8. My favorite meal is a ham and cheese sandwich pickles and milk.

9. No, I don't need a nail hammer or glue.

10. Annabelle packed a blanket a picnic lunch and a croquet set.

Read each sentence. Add commas to separate the coordinate adjectives.

11. The fastest tallest roller coaster at the amusement park is called the Screaming Serpent.

12. We adopted an energetic adorable kitten from the animal shelter.

13. Aunt Lucy helped me choose a safe reliable bike for my commute to school.

14. Griffin bought sturdy green boots for his camping trip to the rain forest.

15. The thin chewy crust on Dad's pizza was our family's favorite.

Read each sentence. Use commas to separate the independent clauses.

16. Sophie wants to ski but she injured her ankle.

17. I want to sleep late so I'll shut off my phone.

18. I like the gadget but I already own one.

19. Dylan will grab dinner on the way home or you can cook.

20. Elliot had such a good time at the musical and he's still talking about it.

For additional help, review pages 614–617 in your textbook or visit www.voyagesinenglish.com.

LESSON

4   Idioms

Idioms are words, phrases, or clauses in which the literal meaning differs from the actual meaning.

Read each sentence and circle the idiom.

1. Don't count on him, as he can be a fair-weather friend.

2. Justin ran to the store as quick as lightning.

3. Please don't horse around as you wait in line.

4. A little bird told me that you're trying out for the race.

5. After the all-day track meet, the twins came home and hit the hay.

Read each phrase. Complete the idiom, using the hint as a guide.

6. It's raining _____. [hint: heavily]

7. I'm feeling a bit under _____. [hint: ill]

8. Waiting to go onstage, Rocco had butterflies _____. [hint: nervous]

9. Did you really win, or are you pulling _____? [hint: fibbing]

10. After Thalia confessed to eating the cookies, I was _____. [hint: no longer in trouble]

Read each idiom. Describe an instance when you might use it.

11. It takes two to tango. _____

12. Variety is the spice of life. _____

13. What goes around comes around. _____

14. That's water under the bridge. _____

15. Every cloud has a silver lining. _____

16. The grass is always greener on the other side. _____

Write a description of your weekend. Include three idioms.

17. _____

_____

_____

_____

© Loyola Press. Voyages in English   Grade 7

For additional help, review pages 618–621 in your textbook
or visit www.voyagesinenglish.com.

Chapter 11 • 183

Annotating Poetry

Annotating is a way to help better understand poetry. It includes reading the poem, identifying elements, marking special words, and drawing conclusions.

Read Shakespeare's "Sonnet XXIX."

Sonnet "XXIX" by William Shakespeare

When in disgrace with fortune and men's eyes,

I all alone beweep my outcast state,

And trouble deaf heaven with my bootless cries,

And look upon myself, and curse my fate,

Wishing me like to one more rich in hope,

Featured like him, like him with friends possessed,

Desiring this man's art, and that man's scope,

With what I most enjoy contented least;

Yet in these thoughts my self almost despising,

Haply I think on thee, and then my state,

(Like to the lark at break of day arising

From sullen earth) sings hymns at heaven's gate;

For thy sweet love remembered such wealth brings

That then I scorn to change my state with kings.

Mark three interesting or confusing words and explain their meaning.

1. _____

2. _____

3. _____

Identify and explain these elements.

4. audience: _____

5. figurative language: _____

6. purpose: _____

_____

© Loyola Press. Voyages in English   Grade 7

For additional help, review pages 622–625 in your textbook or visit www.voyagesinenglish.com